BEGINNING OLD-TIME FIDDLE

by Alan Kaufman

Dedication

This book is for my family: Sol, Rose, and Harvey Kaufman, who were there giving generously of their love and assistance at times when I needed it most.

Acknowledgements

Many thanks to: Tony Trischka—my good buddy and favorite zoo attendant, Tim Newcomb—for his talent and patience, Evan Stover, Steve Uhrik, Hank Sapoznik, Bob Carlin, John Jeffords, Jeff McKenzie, Paul Friedman, Beth Goldman, Bob "Big Paws" Jones, Ellen Green—the Comma Queen, and Lisa.

Special thanks to the Rounder Collective, County Records, and those great folks at the John Edwards Memorial Foundation: Paul Wells, Michael Mendelson and Rebecca Ziegler for making this book possible.

Oak Publications
New York ° London ° Sydney

Contents

Copyright © 1977 by Oak Publications,
A Division of Embassy Music Corporation, New York, NY.

Order No. OK 63503
International Standard Book Number: 0.8256.0308.0
Library of Congress Catalog Card Number: 76-50483

Exclusive Distributors:

Music Sales Corporation
257 Park Avenue South, New York, NY 10010 USA
Music Sales Limited
8/9 Frith Street, London W1V 5TZ England
Music Sales Pty. Limited
120 Rothschild Street, Rosebery, Sydney NSW 2018 Australia

Illustrations by Tim Newcomb
Cover design by Iris Weinstein
Book design by Iris Weinstein and Barbara Hoffman

Photo Credits:
pages 5, 6, 35, 49, 57, 59, 69   courtesy of John Edwards
                                            Memorial Foundation
pages 8, 23, 27, 50, 71, 75, 96, 102   Carl Fleischhauer
pages 11, 33, 65, 79   David Gahr
page 45   Margo Rosenbaum
page 82   Ray Alden
page 91   Doug Conner
page 92   Alan Jabbour

Printed in the United States of America by
Vicks Lithograph and Printing Corporation

Introduction

This book was written with the beginner in mind. It's designed to answer most of the questions a beginner might ask. No prior knowledge of the fiddle or of old-time playing is needed to learn from these pages.

However, more advanced players may also wish to use it as a collection of fine old tunes with which to further expand their repertoires.

The information contained in this book will provide you with a solid foundation in all the basics of old-time fiddling technique. You can put it to its best use as a supplement to the knowledge gained by listening to and watching other fiddlers play.

It might take you a while to assimilate all the ideas expressed here. Work at your own pace. Depending on how busy a person you are, you may have plenty of time to devote to your fiddling interest, or on the other hand you may be restricted to a few precious hours a week. Organize a schedule of practice that suits your own lifestyle and try to be consistent with it.

You will be surprised how really easy it is to learn to play old-time fiddle. This may seem hard to believe, in light of the many myths suggesting that the world of the beginning fiddler is one of much struggling and frustration. But keep in mind that if you adopt the right kind of attitude virtually nothing can stop you from becoming a fine old-time fiddler.

You will become pretty satisfied with your progress if you continue to work at it—and keep smiling. No matter how difficult a particular technique appears at first, approach it with an aura of confidence and you will soon master it.

The initial inspiration to write this book came from a few friends of mine who asked me to recommend a book from which they could learn to play fiddle. Although I knew of some fine advanced instruction books, I couldn't locate any which catered to the needs of the beginner. I tried to help fill this gap by preparing a series of brief instructive articles on basic fiddling technique, which would be submitted to one of the folk music magazines for publication. After drawing up a lengthy outline for this series, it occured to me that I already had enough material to fill up an entire book. Now, three years and many sleepless nights of typing later, this long-awaited beginner's guide is at your disposal. Use it well, for it was meant to be used. The many concepts discussed at length throughout the book will help you to further appreciate the wisdom of the old-time fiddler.

History

Old-Time Fiddling can be defined as the backwoods style from which emerged Western Swing, Country and Western, and Bluegrass fiddling. As an old-timer once explained to me: "Back then we just called it fiddle music. . .nothing more. . .nothing less. Then later on they needed something to tell it apart from the more modern types of fiddling, so they called it old-time fiddling, as good a name as any, I guess."

In the days of the covered wagons, fiddlers were constantly in demand for dances, weddings, christenings, and numerous other social functions. It was quite common for whole communities to gather together for quiltings, barn raisings, molasses making, and husking bees, after which there would be spirited dancing to the sawing of fiddlers until the wee hours of the morning.

Rural families were largely self-sufficient; they grew their own food, made their own clothes, and provided their own entertainment. It was a rare family that wasn't busting at the seams with fiddlers and banjo players. Tunes, like the fiddles they were played on, were handed down from one generation to the next within the family unit. The following recollections are those of James Sievers of the original Tennessee Ramblers, who recorded in 1928-1930:

> *"Actually our dad taught us everything we knew about old-time music. He'd tell us he learned it from his grandfather. As far back as we can remember there's been an instrument in the Siever family. My father's grandfather played fiddle, my uncle played banjo, and my grandmother played the fiddle—and each one could dance. It stayed in the family."†*

The first fiddler to be recorded on a phonograph disc was A.C. "Eck" Robertson of Amarillo, Texas. While attending the 1922 Old Confederate Soldiers' Reunion in Richmond, Virginia, Eck met Henry Gilliland, fiddler and Confederate veteran. They must have enjoyed each others' playing, for they decided to meet in New York City the following month to audition for the Victor Talking Machine Company. I can just imagine the look on the faces of the Victor recording technicians when Eck, dressed in full cowboy regalia, and Henry, sporting a Confederate soldier's uniform, entered the recording studio.

During the first session they recorded "Arkansas Traveller" and "Turkey in the Straw." On these tunes, Henry lined out the basic melody while Eck added a high harmony part to it. The following day, Eck recorded four more tunes, this time without Gilliland. On two of these recordings he was accompanied by a pianist supplied by the studio (the other two were unaccompanied fiddle solos). One of these was his now legendary rendition of "Sally Goodin," which has yet to be equalled. This "Sally Goodin" (written as "Sallie Gooden" on the record label) with "Arkansas Traveller" on the flip side, was released on September 1, 1922, and thus became the first commercially recorded phonograph disc of any fiddler. What is even more startling is that it was also the very first commercial recording of *any* country musician!

†*Old Time Music* **No. 13, Summer 1964, p 6**

During the next ten years, many other great fiddlers were to follow in Eck's footsteps, recording tunes from their repertoires and thus preserving them for future generations of fiddling enthusiasts.

Charlie Bowman, Lowe Stokes, and Fiddlin' John Carson are but a few of the fiddlers who gained widespread popularity by virtue of their commercial recordings.

By the mid-1930s, as a result of the decline in sales brought on by the Depression, most record companies had dropped the "old time" category from their catalogues. This brought to a close a brief yet prolific era of commercially recorded old time fiddling.

More recently, small companies such as County Records and The Rounder Collective have taken on the task of reissuing many of the old classic recordings, once again making them available to the public.

It's pretty amazing if you stop to think that you can put on a record and hear Fiddlin' John Carson as he sounded in 1925.

These days old time fiddling is once again rising in popularity. Fiddle contests throughout the country are drawing larger and larger audiences with each passing year. All across the nation young fiddlers are busy collecting and learning tunes from other fiddlers, thus becoming aware of our great musical heritage.

A.C. "Eck" Robertson

Getting Started: Listening

Before you begin to actually play fiddle tunes, you must first develop a feeling for them by listening to them. Listen to as many old-time fiddle records as you can get your hands on. (For those who don't as yet own any fiddle records, see Appendix 8 for a list of recommended records and record distributors.)

Another way to get involved in the spirit of fiddling is by attending fiddle contests and folk festivals. This is a great way to learn tunes and meet some outstanding fiddlers. If you haven't already done so, by all means go to one. A comprehensive list of these events can be obtained by writing to the Library of Congress's Archive of Folk Song.

Don't worry if after the first two or three weeks, you still don't sound like a fiddler. The more you *listen* and try to *play what you hear*—the better fiddler you'll become.

Give yourself enough room in which to practice—a few feet of unobstructed space all around you should be sufficient. If you prefer to sit while you fiddle, as I do, use an armless chair. And, whenever possible, try to practice in front of a full-length mirror.

Bill Hopkins

Some Preliminary Notes About Your Instrument

First check out your fiddle.* Compare it to the drawing below. Make sure it's all there! Bear in mind that a violin and a fiddle are physically the same instrument; the only difference is the style in which it is played.

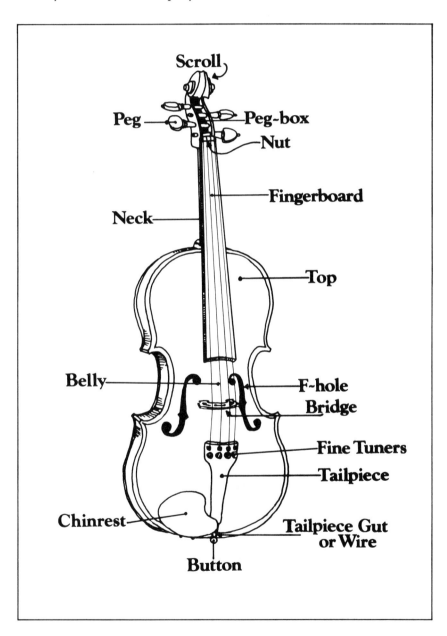

*If you haven't already acquired a fiddle and bow, turn to Appendix I, p.103 for some helpful suggestions on how to go about it. See also Appendices II and IV for further information on caring for your instrument and changing strings.

Positioning of the Bridge

The feet of your bridge† should be in line with the innermost notches of the F-holes of your fiddle. Most fiddles have two markings on the belly to guide you in making this adjustment.

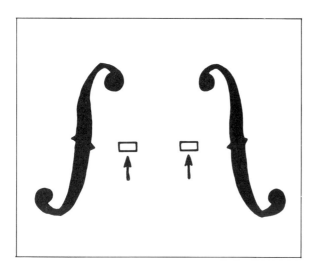

In the event that you have to move your bridge be sure to loosen the tension on all the strings before you begin to reposition it.

Strings

Most fiddlers use steel strings. A few good brands to try are Thomastic, Prim, and Super Sensitive. Any of these will do for a start. Later on, you might want to experiment around to find the brand that best complements the sound of your fiddle.

Pop Hafler (fiddle) and Les Parsons 1974

†Keep in mind that bridges on fiddles, unlike those found on most fretted instruments, should never be glued to the instrument.

Tuning

Tuning your fiddle may be a little tricky at first, but keep at it. The more experience you have with tuning, the easier it becomes.

Sit yourself down in a quiet room and hold the fiddle on your lap with the button resting on your knees. Then place the fingers of your right hand around the base of the neck, as in the illustration below, while keeping the thumb of your right hand free and adjacent to the strings. Now grasp the G string peg with the thumb and index finger of your left hand. You're now in position to tune up the G string.

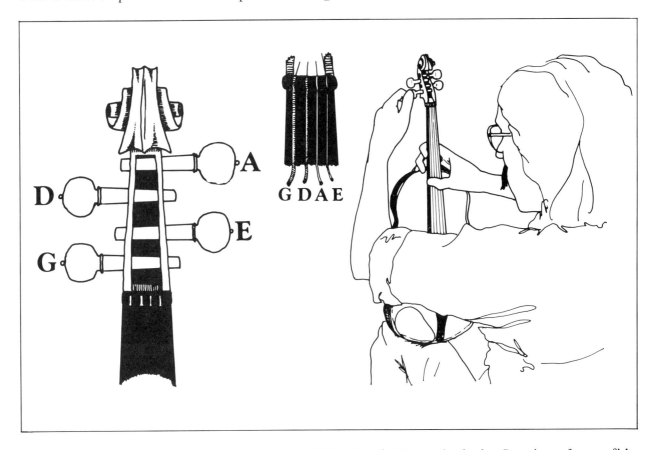

Listen to the 2nd band on the soundsheet ("Tuning"). Then pluck the G string of your fiddle with the thumb of your right hand and compare it to the G on the record. Now, turn the G string peg *very slowly* with your left hand *as you pluck* the string with your right thumb until you reach the note matching the sound on the recording. (Turning the peg without plucking is a sure way to break a string.) When you get to where the note sounds right, push the peg into the pegbox. This will prevent the string from slipping out of tune.

The pegs on some older fiddles can often be quite troublesome. They may for reasons of excessive wear or improper fit be either hard to turn, or very difficult to keep from slipping. If the latter is your problem, take the string off the peg and remove the peg from the pegbox; then coat (sparingly) the stem of the peg with blackboard chalk or fiddle rosin. This should effectively remedy the problem.

If on the other hand your pegs are hard to turn, try greasing with a lubricant. Hill peg lubricant, which is distributed by the Hill Company of London, is the best product of this type I've yet come across. You can get it through your local violin dealer or repairman.

Keep in mind that the bridge on your fiddle should be almost perpendicular to the belly, leaning only very slightly toward the tailpiece.

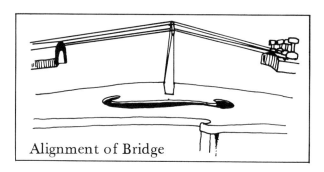
Alignment of Bridge

If, as you tune, you notice the bridge leaning quite a bit in either direction, readjust it. Try to get yourself into the habit of checking the alignment of your bridge regularly—especially while tuning.

Now recheck your G with the one on the soundsheet. If it's slightly out of tune, use your *fine tuner.* This is a metal screw device that fits onto your tailpiece. Fine tuners enable you to make those very fine adjustments often necessary for hitting the note right on the button. All fiddles equipped with steel strings should have a set of four fine tuners, one for each string. They're very inexpensive and can be purchased at most music stores.

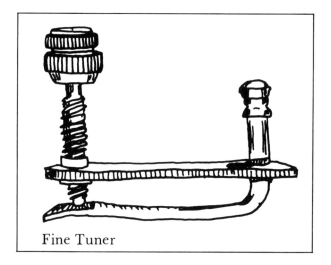
Fine Tuner

Also available and highly recommended, though more costly, is the Thomastic tailpiece. This is an all-metal tailpiece with four built-in fine tuners.

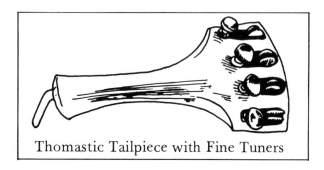
Thomastic Tailpiece with Fine Tuners

Regardless of the type you have, fine tuners all work the same way. Turning the screw in a clockwise direction raises the pitch while turning it counter-clockwise lowers it.

Never let the bottom of the fine tuner mechanism come in contact with the belly of the fiddle. I've seen too many fiddles permanently scarred by people careless with their fine tuners.

If the G string is still too far out of range to be corrected with the aid of your fine tuner, then try the peg once more.

Now, follow the same procedure with the D string (i.e., listen to the example of the D on the soundsheet, pluck your D string, compare pitches, etc.)

To tune the A and E strings, simply reverse hands, with your right hand controlling the peg and your left thumb plucking the string.

Don't expect perfection on your first try; precision in tuning comes with experience and perseverance.*

Maria (D'Amato) Muldaur

*For more on tuning, see Appendix III, p. 104.

Holding the Fiddle

There is no *right* way to hold your fiddle and bow. Fiddlers learn these skills by imitating other fiddlers and then experimenting on their own until they find a way that's both efficient and comfortable.

You may find it best to sample each of the following three methods and then choose the one best suited to your needs.

Many old time fiddlers hold their instruments as I'm holding mine in the drawing below:

To hold the neck of the fiddle, place your index finger on the right side of the fingerboard with your thumb on the left. The index finger should meet the neck between the 1st joint (where the finger meets the hand) and the middle joint. The thumb should be directly across the fingerboard from the index finger. Under no circumstances should the fiddle neck rest in the place where the thumb joins the hand.

Some fiddlers employ a straightened-out wrist when holding their fiddles, as is illustrated below. This technique comes in handy with many Texas-style tunes, where variations played all the way up the neck are quite common. This method also makes it easier to note with the fourth finger of your left hand. Therefore, those of you with very short fingers should give it a serious try.

If you have trouble holding your fiddle under your chin, trying using a shoulder rest. Most larger music stores have several models of these in stock similar to the one pictured below:

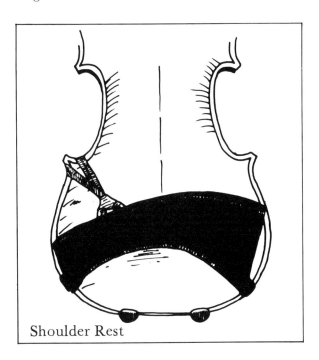

Shoulder Rest

If you're a little short on money, you can construct one easily and cheaply, using only a sponge and a rubber band, as follows: Place a sponge on the back of your fiddle, positioned so that it's directly opposite the chinrest. Then use a rubber band to hold it in place, connecting one end of the band to the button and hooking the other onto the points on the right side of the fiddle (the same side the chinrest is on).

Still some other fiddlers hold their instruments in what is my own favorite way—on the chest.

Supporting the Fiddle on Your Chest

This position, which I have found to be the most relaxing of them all, gives you the freedom to sing and play your fiddle at the same time.

The Bow

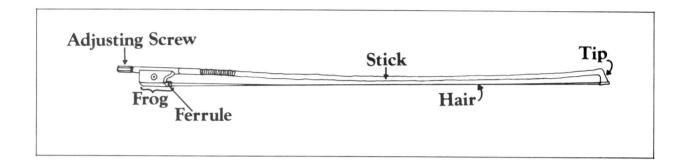

Tightening the Bow

Before your bow can be of any use to you it must be properly tightened. To accomplish this, turn the adjusting screw on the bow in a clockwise direction. It should be tight enough so that none of the hairs touch the stick as you play.

To be safe, tighten it *gradually* and test it by playing on any string. The bow will be properly tightened when with the application of slight pressure the hair no longer touches the stick. Avoid tightening it much further past this point, as excessive tension has been known to cause bows to snap right in half.

When loosened, the stick of your bow should have a noticeable arch to it. As you tighten it, be careful that the arch doesn't totally straighten out. If it does, then you're probably tightening it too much.

During the course of playing it is quite normal to have a few hairs break off your bow, especially if you have a heavy touch. When this breakage gets to be excessive, take your bow to a violin maker/repairman to have it rehaired. Bear in mind that it might take a few days or a week before you get your bow back. For this reason it is advisable to have two bows, so that you have one to play with while the other is being rehaired.

One final note: Always loosen your bow before putting it away.

Rosin

If you were to observe a strand of hair under high magnification, you would see a long filament with many barbs or hooks attached to it. When you draw your bow across a string, the hooks on the bow hair catch onto the string, setting it vibrating. This in turn sets the air in the body of the instrument vibrating and thereby produces sound.

When you rosin your bow, you're coating the hair with a tacky substance, thus making it more effective in grabbing onto the string.

New cakes of rosin have a shiny surface. It helps to roughen up this surface with a key or some other sharp object before using it. This makes the rosin easier to apply. A few good brands of rosin are: Hill, Hidersine, and Thomastic.

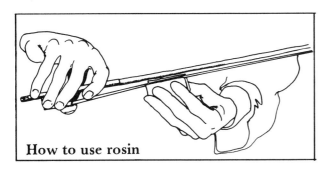

How to use rosin

Hold the bow as in the above drawing, with your thumb underneath the frog, covering the ferrule, so as not to chip or break your rosin on the metal end of the frog. Then, holding the rosin stationary, move the bow hair over the rosin from the frog to the tip and back, applying slight pressure with the right-hand index finger.

How much rosin to apply is a matter of the individual fiddler's preference. A half-dozen strokes' worth of rosin for every few hours of fiddling should do the trick. New bows, or newly rehaired ones, usually require more rosin.

Some old time fiddlers let the rosin dust accumulate on the bellies of their fiddles. A Virginia fiddler once told me that he does it for "protection"—so that when times get hard again, he can use it as an emergency supply until he can afford a new cake.

Other fiddlers feel that this accumulation of rosin improves the sound of their instruments.

Holding the Bow

A few of the many varied ways old timers hold their bows are described below:

Place the bow at an angle across the fingers of your right hand, as in the illustration:

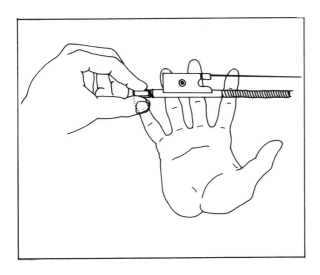

Bend the fingers of your right hand so that they comfortably enclose the bow. Then bend your thumb and place the tip of your thumb against the bottom of the stick (on top in this position) at the edge of the frog.

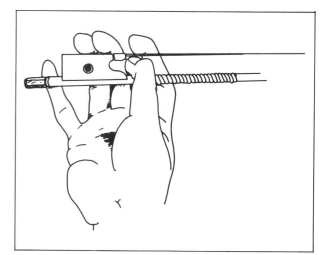

Now, turn the bow around and readjust the position of your right hand, where necessary, so as to conform with that in the drawing:

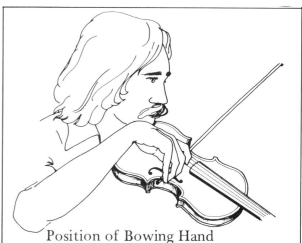

Position of Bowing Hand

Try not to grip your bow too rigidly. You should use only that tension necessary to keep the bow from flying out of your hand.
Some old timers prefer to hold their bows further up on the stick. This is known as "choking up" on the bow.

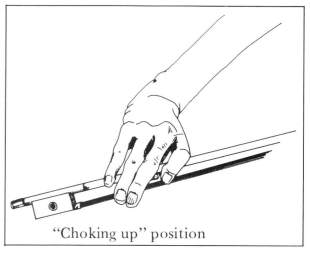

"Choking up" position

Another common method is holding the bow with only the thumb, index, and middle fingers as shown here:

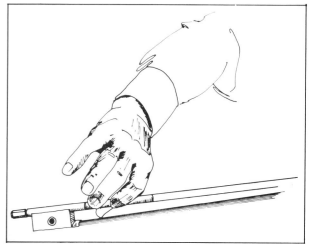

Basic Technique

Right-Hand Awareness: The Bow Stroke

Place your bow on the A string of your fiddle (second string from the right).

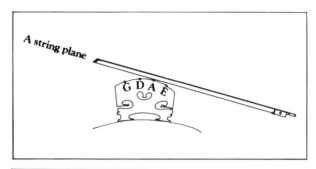

Then, pull the bow across the string from the frog to the tip as in the drawing below. This movement is known as a *downstroke*:

Be sure to keep the movement of the bow confined to the area between the bridge and the end of the fingerboard. At first, you might find it difficult to play on one string without hitting the strings adjacent to it, but keep at it. Once you get accustomed to the curvature of the bridge it will become much easier.

As you finish your downstroke, the tip of the bow should be in contact with the string. This puts you in position for the *upstroke,* which pushes the bow from the tip back to the frog:

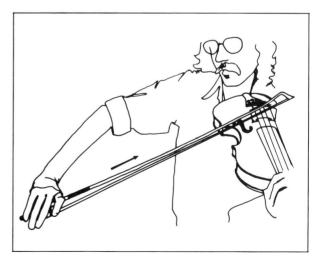

Wrist motion is crucial to bowing. When your hand is in position for a downstroke, as it will be at the end of an upstroke, your wrist should be pointing towards the tip of the bow.

As you follow through on the downstroke, the angle of your wrist should gradually invert so that when you reach the tip of the bow your wrist will point away from the tip.

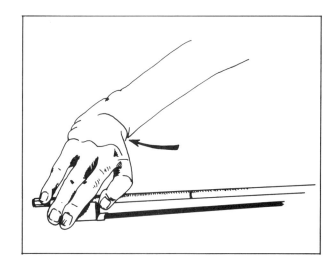

It is really important to try to keep your wrist as loose as possible. This looseness is what makes good fiddling sound super-smooth.

Here are a few exercises to get you warmed up and in shape for those fine old fiddle tunes we'll soon be getting to:

Play a bunch of downstrokes (↓) alternating with upstrokes (↑) on the G string of your fiddle (i.e., downstroke–upstroke–downstroke–upstroke–etc.) and try to keep the tone even and steady from the beginning to the end of each stroke:

<pre>
↓   ↑   ↓   ↑
G   G   G   G,   etc.
</pre>

Be careful that you don't tense up your bowing arm.

Now continue this exercise on the other three strings of your fiddle:

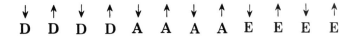

<pre>
↓   ↑   ↓   ↑   ↓   ↑   ↓   ↑   ↓   ↑   ↓   ↑
D   D   D   D   A   A   A   A   E   E   E   E
</pre>

Now start again on the G string with a downstroke followed by an upstroke. Then move the bow onto the next string (D) and repeat the same two bowstrokes. Continue in the same way on to the A and E strings.

↓ ↑ ↓ ↑ ↓ ↑ ↓ ↑
G G D D A A E E

Now try it backwards. Start with the E and work your way toward the G string. As with the exercise above, aim for smoothness and evenness.

↓ ↑ ↓ ↑ ↓ ↑ ↓ ↑
E E A A D D G G

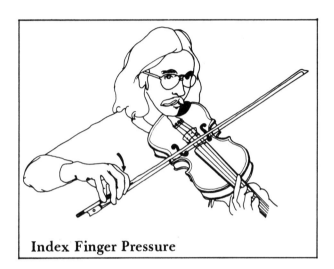

Index Finger Pressure

The index finger of your right hand plays an important role in the development of your bowing technique—by applying slight pressure to the bow with it, you can increase both the volume and clarity of your tone. This subtle pressure should be only slightly more than that supplied by the weight of your hand alone. Don't overdo it, for too much pressure can make your fiddling sound harsh and scratchy.

The weight of a bow is not evenly distributed throughout the stick. As you can see in the drawing below depicting the balance point, much of the weight is concentrated in the lower third of the bow (due in part to the weight of the frog and adjusting screw mechanism).

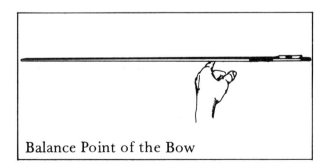

Balance Point of the Bow

In order to achieve a smooth, even tone throughout your bowstrokes, you must compensate for this difference in weight. This is accomplished by *increasing* the index-finger pressure on the downstroke *as you reach the tip* and then gradually *decreasing* on the upstroke *as you get closer to the frog.* This technique especially comes in handy when you're playing tunes in the *long bow style,* also called "Texas style," in which there are several notes played on each bowstroke, thus requiring long bowstrokes.

One last point: Remember to keep your wrist loose. Try not to tense up, relax.

Left-Hand Awareness: Finger Patterns

With your fiddle held like a guitar, pluck the open (unfingered) D string with your right-hand thumb. Think of this note as the *Do,* or first note of a major scale (Do—Re—Mi—Fa—So—La—Ti—Do).

Next, place the tip of your left-hand index finger on the D string and, plucking the string with your thumb, try to find the note that best approximates the *Re* note (as in Do—Re—Mi etc).

Your finger should be arched, with the tip perpendicular to the fingerboard of the fiddle. Be sure that your fingertip is confined to the D string only; in this way you can avoid interfering with any of the adjacent strings. You may find it hard to use the tips of your fingers if your fingernails are long, so cut them if necessary.

To produce the Re note, the index finger should be positioned approximately 1¼"† from the nut on the D string.

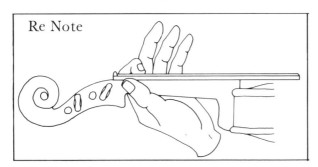

Keep in mind that if your instrument isn't set up correctly, the Re note may deviate considerably from the approximate distance given here. Check to see if your bridge is properly positioned (see "Positioning of the Bridge," p. 8).

†**All of these measurements are for full size (4/4) fiddles only!**

Now, while keeping your index finger down on the Re space, place your middle finger on the spot that best approximates the *Mi* sound and pluck the string. The middle finger should be about 1-1/8″ from the first finger of the left hand.

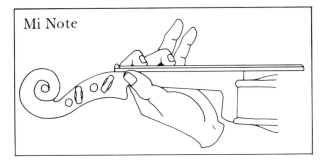

Now, while keeping your first two fingers down on the string, place your ring finger next to the middle finger, as in the drawing below.* The plucked note should sound like the *Fa* or fourth note of the major scale.

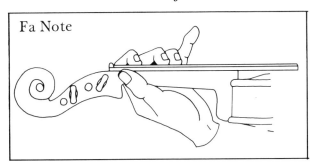

Now, keeping your first three fingers (up to Fa) down on the string, stretch your pinky to the *So* note and pluck it.

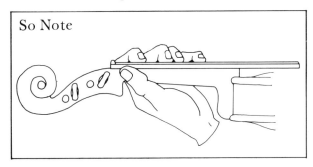

If you find that you are having trouble extending your pinky that far, don't worry. With the passing of time your pinky, as well as your other left-hand fingers, will become stronger and more flexible. If at this point you can only go comfortably as far as the third finger, that's fine for now; we won't be playing tunes that require the use of the fourth finger until later on in the book anyway.

Now let's try putting all this stuff together:

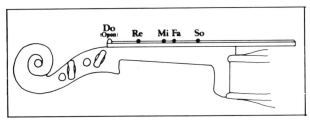

Pluck the open D string. . . . . **Do**
Pluck the first fingered note . . . . **Re**
Pluck the second fingered note . . . . **Mi**
Pluck the third fingered note. . . . . **Fa**
Pluck the fourth fingered note . . . . **So**

*How close these two fingers actually are to each other depends, of course, on the size of your hand and the thickness of your fingers.

Now repeat the above exercise, this time using the bow. Play each note on a separate bow-stroke, starting on a downstroke. Keep each consecutive finger down on the string so that when you reach the fourth-fingered note all four fingers are down in place on the string. You can check your results with the example found on the sound-sheet which accompanies the text.

Study the pattern that the four fingers of your left hand have made on the fingerboard. This is the *first finger pattern,* or FP1.

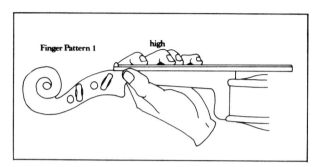

The study of finger patterns provides a quick and easy way to familiarize yourself with the fingerboard of your fiddle. All in all, there are five finger patterns, three of which are presented here. We'll be getting to the other two later on in the text. Try to have these finger patterns committed to memory as soon as you can. To get the most out of the tunes in this book, your knowledge of them should become second nature.

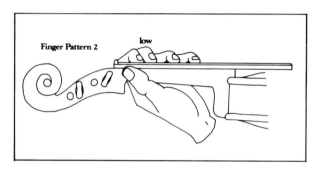

Finger Pattern 2 (FP2) is only slightly different from the first finger pattern. The first, third, and fourth fingers are in exactly the same location as in FP1. The only change is in the placement of the second finger, which now is close to the first. If there is a large space between the first and second fingers, with the second finger close to the third (as in FP1), then the second finger is in *high position.* If the first and second fingers are close together with a large space between the second and third fingers, as in FP2, then the second finger is in *low position* ("low" because, being closer to the nut, it's lower in pitch).

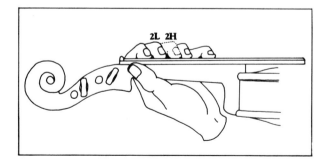

This lowered finger alters the relationship of the notes to each other, so that FP2 does not correspond to the beginning of the major scale (Do–Re–Mi–Fa–So) as FP1 does.

Now try plucking each of the notes in the second finger pattern (starting on the open D string). Then, bow through the FP2 sequence as you did with **FP1**, using separate bow-strokes, starting on a downstroke. You can use the soundsheet as a guide.

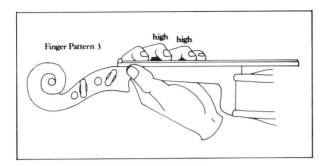

Finger Pattern 3 (FP3) is very similar to **FP1**. The first, second and fourth fingers are the same (second finger in high position). However, the third finger is in high position, close to the fourth finger. As with the two previous patterns, first pluck through this note sequence until you get a basic feel for it, then bow it, checking it with the soundsheet.

Tablature

Beginners will find that tablature provides a simple and easy approach to learning tunes. Once you become familiar with the workings of fiddle tab you can have a few solid tunes under your belt in no time at all. To get the most out of these tablatures, you should use them in conjunction with a recorded source. For example, when you're ready to begin working out the first tune, "Sally Goodin," listen to the version on the soundsheet first. Then use the tablature as a guide to help you communicate the tune to your hands.

How to Read It

The *four spaces* in the fiddle tab staff each represent one of the four strings of the fiddle.

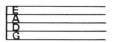

The *numbers* in the spaces refer to the fingers of your left hand. The zeros refer to open (unfingered) strings.

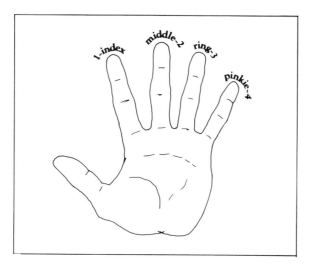

The **H** above the 2 in the example below indicates a high second finger (as in FP1), while an **L** above a note indicates a low finger position.

In "Sally Goodin," the first note, shown below by $\frac{H}{2}$, lies on the space second from the top. This note, then, is played with the second finger of your left hand on the A string. The next note is an open A string.

The lines (*stems*) beneath the numbers refer to rhythm. These rhythm symbols are the same in standard notation and the fiddle tab. They indicate the duration of the notes—how long each note is held. The temporal relationship of these notes to each other is illustrated by the pyramid below:

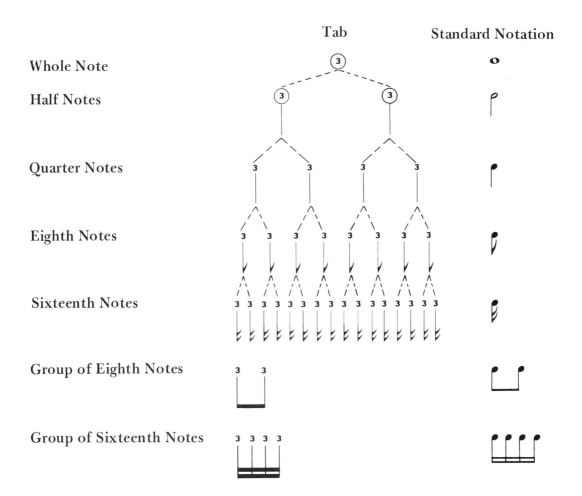

Groups of two or more eighth notes are most often connected by a horizontal line (a *beam*).

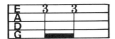

Two or more sixteenth notes are connected by two of these beams.

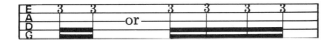

You may ask, how long is a quarter note? How many seconds do I hold it? Think of two pies, one large and one small, cut into quarters:

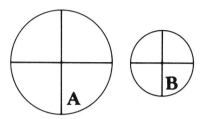

Although slice A is much larger than slice B, they are each one quarter of a pie. The fraction here is relative. How large the quarter slice is depends on how large the whole pie is. The same is true in music: The length of a quarter note depends on the length you assign to the whole note.

In tab, as in standard notation, notes are beamed together in clusters each of which equals one beat. In most cases a quarter note—or its equivalent in other notes—equals one beat.

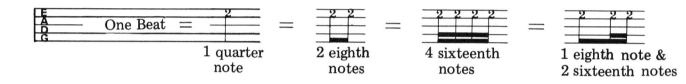

| 1 quarter note | 2 eighth notes | 4 sixteenth notes | 1 eighth note & 2 sixteenth notes |

In "Sally Goodin," below, the notes are arranged in groups of two beats. These groupings, called *measures,* are separated by vertical lines known as *bar lines*:

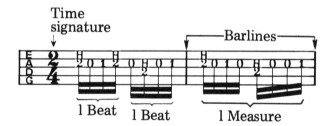

The symbol 2/4 at the left of the first staff line of music means that the music contains *two quarter-note beats per measure.* This symbol is called the *time signature.* Tunes using this symbol are said to be "in 2/4 time."

The strongest accent should always fall on the first note of each measure. To properly accent or emphasize these notes, apply some pressure to the bow with your index finger (see "Right Hand Awareness" p. 17).

Some fiddle tunes have a few notes preceding the first complete measure. These notes are known as the *upbeat.* Upbeats (also called pickup notes) can serve to tie together the beginnings and endings of tunes, thus giving them their distinctive cyclical feel.

Most fiddle tunes are composed of two parts of equal length, known as the A and B parts; each part is repeated twice (AABB).

The symbols for the *repeat* are 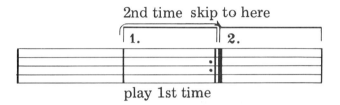. All notes contained within these symbols should be repeated before moving on to the next part. If the repeated section starts at the very beginning of the tune, the left-hand part of the repeat symbol is omitted.

Some tunes have repeated parts that are played somewhat differently the second time around at the end. In this case, play the measure marked ⌐1. the first time through, but when making the repeat, substitute for it the measure marked ⌐2. .

Ira Mullins of Clay County, West Va. (fiddle) and Phoeba Parsons of Orma, West Va. (fiddlesticks)

Keys and Key Signatures

A key is a specific set of notes from which tunes are constructed, with a main note which is the key center. Usually the tune will end with that note.

When a fiddler says, "This tune is in the key of G," he means that this tune consists of notes drawn from a set known as the key of G.

The chart below shows the notes in the key of G as they appear on the fingerboard of a fiddle.

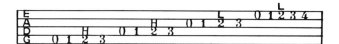

Notice that the G and D Strings each consist of notes drawn from the *first finger pattern* (high second finger), whereas the A and E strings contain the notes from the *second finger pattern* (low second finger).

With this in mind, an easy way to remember the key of G is:

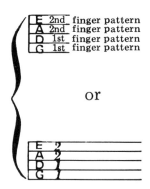

The abbreviation shown above is the *fiddle tab key signature.* It is found to the right of the title of each tune in this book, and indicates what key the tune is in, as well as what finger patterns will be used on each string in that key.

The tab key signature for the key of D is:

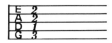

The tab key signature for the key of A is:

28

First Tune: Sally Goodin

When you're trying to learn a tune you should center your consciousness as much as you possibly can on that tune: whistle it, dance to it, try to sing it. If it doesn't have any words—make up your own. Let your whole body rejoice in it. I guess that is what is meant by learning a tune *by heart.* This reminds me of the words of the great fiddler and banjo player from Saltville, Virginia, Hobart Smith:

> *I've been to the cornfield many of a time when I was a farmer and I'd hear a good fiddle tune or a good banjer piece and I'd commence whistlin' it. I'd go pretty far and I'd whistle all the way into the holler of the mountain, and my banjer would be hangin' on the wall. Sometimes I'd forget where I was and I'd whistle right loud and that banjer would answer me on the wall—and I'd go and get her. I'd keep that tune on my mind—and I'd find that tune on the strings before I'd quit*[†] . . .

An easy way to learn tunes off records is by listening to them at a slower speed. At 16 rpm, your 33 1/3 rpm records will sound twice as slow (easier to follow) and in the same key as at 33 1/3, but an octave lower in pitch. If your turntable isn't equipped with 16 rpm, try using a tape recorder. Record the tunes at 7 1/2 ips and play them back at 3 3/4 ips.

Now listen to the recording of "Sally Goodin" on the soundsheet (Side 1/Band 9).

This version of "Sally Goodin" is in the key of A. Do you remember which finger patterns we use for the key of A? If not, check with the fiddle tab key signature at the top of the tune.

Using the transcribed version that follows, pluck through the tune a few times until you get a feel for it. Then try bowing it slowly. You may find that tapping your foot to the beat helps you to keep your timing even.

Notice that the notes in this transcription are all sixteenth notes. Therefore, each note is held for the same time value as the next. Remember, each group of four sixteenth notes is equal to one beat.

Make sure you accent the first note in each of the two beats per measure. The slash marks beneath the notes will help to remind you which notes to emphasize.

As you play, try to keep all your fingers in position on the string—until they are needed elsewhere. In this manner, any finger held down in place can be used as a guide for the following note. Avoiding unnecessary raising and lowering of the fingers will serve to make the noting of the tune a bit easier.

The arrows above the notes indicate whether they are to be played as downstrokes (↓) or upstrokes (↑). This particular bowing style, consisting of a pattern of alternating downstrokes and upstrokes, is known traditionally as the *saw stroke,* or *jig style bowing.* When playing tunes in the saw stroke style, use only the top third of your bow.

[†]*Devil's Box,* **Sept. '73, p. 18**

When you get to the end of a fiddle tune repeat back to the beginning, and then continue to play through the tune as many times as you like.

You've got to get the tune on your mind and then find it with your fingers. Keep on till you find what you want on that neck. But keep that tune in your mind just like you can hear it a-playin'.

—Hobart Smith

Sally Goodin

Fiddle Tab Key Signature:

A Part

B Part

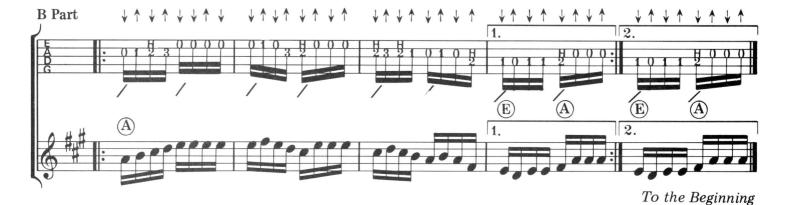

To the Beginning

Had a piece of pie,
Had a piece of puddin',
Gave it all away
For to see my Sally Goodin.

Whenever you come across notes that sound out of tune, take the time out to correct them. At first they may include most of the notes you play—but never fear, if you persevere in correcting errors you will have the tune sounding fine in no time at all.

Be honest with yourself. Don't go on to any other tunes until you have this one down to your satisfaction.

Troubleshooting

Playing Problems

Now that you've gotten through your first tune, take some time to work the kinks out of your playing. Some of the most common problems which beginners face are discussed below:

Tone

Poor tone is often caused by gripping the bow too rigidly. Also, playing too close to the bridge tends to make a fiddle squeak a lot.

Once you start to feel more at home with the techniques of bowing, you'll find that your tone will begin to sound quite a bit better, so just hang in there.

Rhythm

Remember, fiddle music is primarily dance music, and to play for a dance you've got to have rhythm steady as a rock. When practicing tunes, make an extra-special effort to keep your timing steady. Don't try to play super-fast right away. You'll get there in time, but for now, work at playing slowly and clearly. Try to play the tunes only as fast as you can play their most difficult sections. In this way you can avoid the necessity of playing slower when you get to the tough parts.

The beat is the lifeline, the pulse of a fiddle tune. Without it all you have left is a monotonous string of notes. Be sure to emphasize the beat in all your tunes.

Cramped hands/finger fatigue

Once your hands begin to feel tired or cramped, stop and relax! If you continue to play, you will just be wasting energy and possibly doing some harm to your body.

One surefire way to gain instant relief is by shaking out your hands; shake your wrist loosely in circles, while keeping your fingers free as if you're shaking water off your hands.

Instrument Problems

Here are some common instrument problems which you might be confronted with:

Buzzes

If your strings are too high off the fingerboard, you will have a hard time trying to press them down. If they are too low, they will probably buzz. The distance between the strings and the fingerboard at the nut should be equivalent to the thickness of an ordinary playing card.

If either of these problems affects your instrument, don't attempt to fix it yourself unless absolutely sure you know what you're doing. You would do well to go to a reputable instrument repairman, preferably one recommended by the fiddlers in your area.

Besides the height of the strings, the most likely cause of buzzing is a loose screw on one of your fine tuners. You can fix this yourself pretty easily just by tightening the screw. Old strings may also be responsible for weird buzzes. It's best not to wait for them to break; change them as soon as they start getting old and rusty.

If it still buzzes and none of the above seems to apply, chances are there's something loose on the inside. At this point there's nothing you can do except bring it to an instrument repairman and have it looked over thoroughly.

Too much/Too little rosin

If you have too much rosin on your bow your fiddling might tend to sound somewhat scratchy, while if your bow doesn't have enough rosin, you'll be lucky to get any sound at all.

Neighbors

You should try to practice your fiddling regularly, but sometimes this isn't quite possible. For instance, you might have a baby sleeping in the next room. Or you might be an apartment house dweller with paper-thin walls, fearful that the next time your downstairs neighbor hears your E string he'll start banging on the pipes again. But even for this seemingly hopeless situation there's a simple solution. Try using a mute.

The device pictured below is a mute made entirely of solid cast metal which, when placed on your bridge, should lower the wailing of your fiddle down to a whisper. Even an irate neighbor will be able to sleep through it.

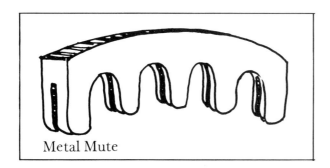

Metal Mute

Here are some other popular mutes. These work primarily by taking the shrillness out of your fiddling.

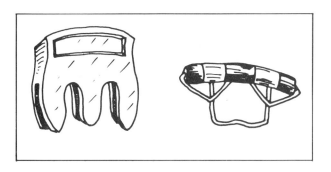

Almeda Riddle and Hobart Smith

Old-Time Fiddle Tunes

Regional Playing Styles

Fiddlers from different parts of the country have their own distinctive styles. For example, "Sally Goodin" as played by a Texas fiddler will sound quite a bit different from that same tune played by a fiddler from North Carolina.

To say that a group of fiddlers play in a specific style means that they play their tunes with similar bowings, rhythms, and ornaments, all of which are common to that particular region.

The growing popularity of fiddle contests in recent years has given rise to a style of its own. This contest-style fiddling is characterized by the use of slick and fancy technique with the emphasis on showmanship.

When watching top-notch fiddlers perform, it's easy to get misdirected into thinking that how good a fiddler is depends upon how dexterous he is with the fingers of his left hand. Bear in mind, though, that the exciting rhythm and enticing tone of a great fiddler are both heavily dependent on the skillful use of his bowing hand.

The Tunes in This Book

The tunes contained in this volume are grouped together by key. Each tune section has at its beginning a small chart showing the finger patterns used in that particular key. Try to commit these charts to memory as soon as you can, for they must become part of you before you can begin to play tunes by ear.

In each section you'll find that the first few tunes are relatively easy; but they get progressively more difficult as you move on.

Following most of the transcriptions, there is a listing of the records on which that particular arrangement is based. I can't over-emphasize the importance of listening. If you really want to learn the tunes you must listen to the records.

Fiddle music sounds especially beautiful when it's accompanied by such instruments as the guitar, the dulcimer, or the piano. For this reason chords have been included along with each tune.

Tunes in the Key of D

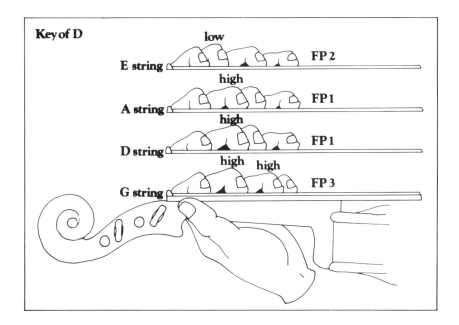

Here's a very simplified version of the old-time tune, "Ida Red." This particular arrangement consists of eighth notes ⌐‾‾⌐ and quarter notes | .

Start this tune on a downstroke and continue onward using the saw-stroke style with alternating bowstrokes. Bowing markings (arrows) have been written out for the first measure to give you the basic idea. Follow this bowing pattern through the remainder of the tune.

Keep in mind that relatively longer notes require longer bowstrokes.

Gid Tanner and The Skillet Lickers

Ida Red

A Part

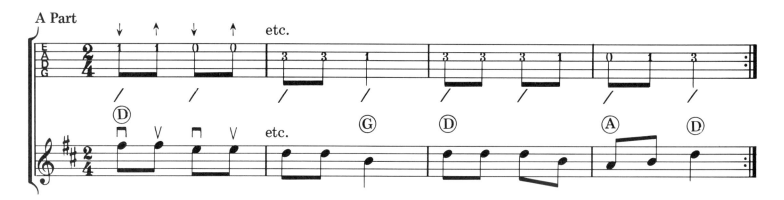

B Part

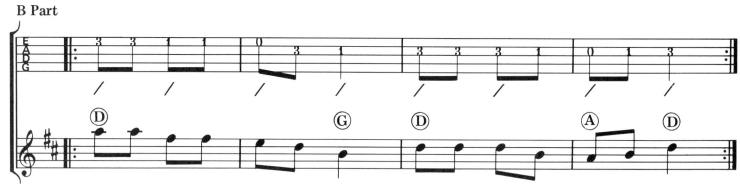

To the Beginning

Shuffle Bowing

"He was one of Kentucky's finest old-time fiddlers. And he had the best shuffle with the bow that I'd ever seen, and kept the best time, that's one reason people asked him to play for dances around Rosine, Kentucky."

These words are those of Bill Monroe, the Father of Bluegrass, and one of the great creative musical geniuses of our time. Here he talks of his Uncle Pen, a fine old fiddler with whom Bill lived while still in his teens.

Throughout time, there have been precious few able to resist the temptation to get up and dance their rears off upon listening to the striking rhythmic strains of a great shuffle fiddler.

The basic unit of a shuffle* is a group of three notes, the first played with a long bowstroke and the following two played with relatively shorter strokes.

*Not to be confused with the shuffle rhythm of blues and rock, an entirely different figure:

Here's what a bunch of shuffle strokes sounds like on the open A string of your fiddle:

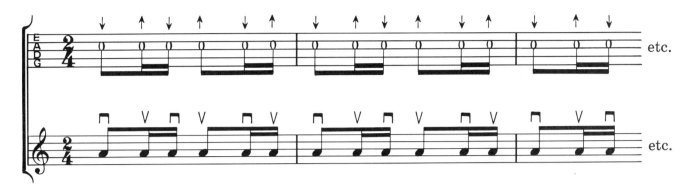

Notice that the bowstroke is continually alternating in direction, first played as a down-stroke, then an upstroke, and so on.

Here's a version of "Ida Red" using shuffle bowing:

Ida Red *(Shuffle Bowing)*

To the Beginning

The Slur

Whenever you have two or more notes played on the same bowstroke, it is indicated in tab by the use of a slur. This is written as a curved line above or below the notes involved.

The eight notes in the example below are slurred together in pairs, and thus we have only half as many bowstrokes as notes. The first two notes are played on a downstroke, the next two on an upstroke, and so on.

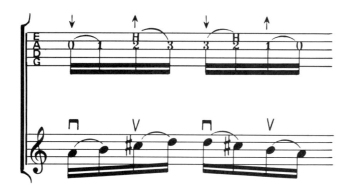

If the notes being slurred are equal in time value, make sure that they are each played with an equal amount of bow.

In this next example, the same phrase is played differently: Only the first pair of notes in each group is slurred, while the next two notes are played on separate strokes.

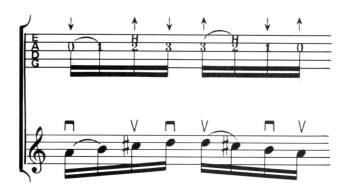

What we have then is, essentially, one long bowstroke followed by two short ones. Sound familiar? It should, for it is your basic shuffle bowing, except that in this case it uses slurred groups of four notes instead of three.

The Eighth Of January

This fine old tune commemorates Andrew Jackson's victory in the Battle of New Orleans. The version transcribed here will provide you with some more good practice in shuffle bowing.

Where slurring is not indicated, continue playing all notes in separate strokes.

A Part

B Part

To the Beginning

The next tune, "Soldier's Joy," one of the most popular of all fiddle tunes, is known in some parts of the country as the "King's Head Reel." The legend goes that a man condemned to die on the gallows had his life spared after playing this tune before the king.

The old-time fiddler can choose from a wide selection of ornaments to dress up his tunes. Among the most basic of these ornaments is the octave note. This can be found by playing the third finger on any given string with the adjacent open string below it, to its left. For example, in the first and second endings of the B part of "Soldier's Joy," the third finger on the A string is played along with the open D.

When playing an octave note, be sure to arch your finger so that it doesn't touch any strings except the ones you're noting.

Soldier's Joy

To the Beginning

Triplets

A group of three notes with the numeral 3 in italics under it is known as a triplet.

A triplet in the form of three sixteenth notes is played in the same time as two ordinary sixteenth notes or one eighth note.

Fiddlers usually play all three of these notes on the same bowstroke.

Triplets are pretty commonly found in Irish, New England, and Texas tunes, but are rarely used by fiddlers in the Southeast. Sometimes they are written as eighth notes, in which case they are equal to two regular eighth notes or a quarter note.

Unison Notes

Provided that your fiddle is reasonably in tune, you can play the same note either by using your fourth finger on any given string, or by playing the adjacent open string above it, to its right. (Obviously, the fourth finger on the E string is an exception to this.) For example, placing your fourth finger in position on the A string should result in a note identical to the open E string.

Playing both these notes together results in what is called a unison note. This embellishment occurs in the fourth measure of the A part in the following arrangement of "Morpeth Rant." In the standard notation this is shown with double stems:

Morpeth Rant

Allan Block and Ralph Lee Smith Meadowlands MS-1

Here's a neat harmony part that I learned from fiddler Paul Friedman:

Morpeth Rant (Harmony Part)

A-PART Harmony

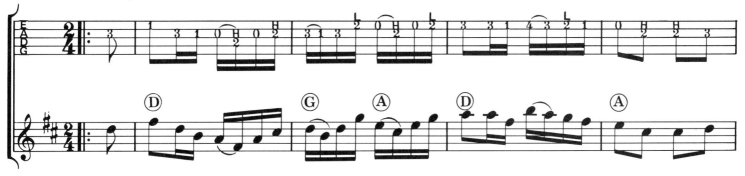

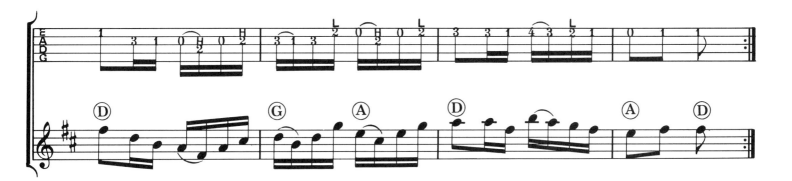

B-PART Harmony

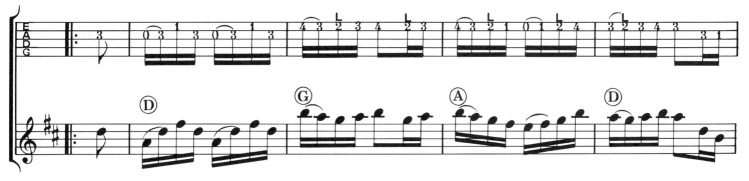

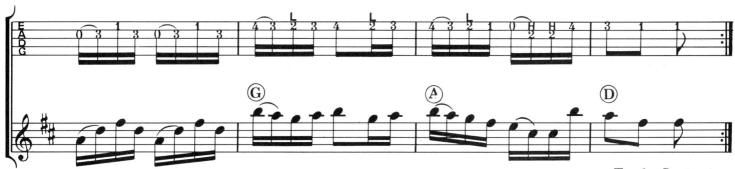

To the Beginning

Keep in mind that each arrangement in this book represents only one way in which the tune can be played. How you will ultimately play the tune depends on your own taste.

Mississippi Sawyer

This particular arrangement combines both shuffle and saw-stroke rhythms.

To the Beginning

Tunes in 6/8 time are known as *jigs*. The symbol 6/8 indicates that there are 6 eighth-note beats (or the equivalent in other notes) per measure. These beats are grouped together in two groups of three each, so the rhythm actually has a feeling of two beats per measure (a piece in 2/4 written in eighth-note triplets would be equivalent). The accent in jigs should be placed on the first note in each group.

In the next tune, "Haste to the Wedding," the last measure of the B part has a quarter note followed by a dot. Whenever a note is followed by a dot, its time value is increased by one-half.

A dotted quarter note,   is thus equal to

Al Murphy and Art Rosenbaum

Haste To The Wedding

As played by Mrs. Ben Scott of Turlock, California.

To the Beginning

American Fiddle Tunes Library of Congress AFS L62

Now that you have some basic fiddling technique behind you, try to put more of yourself into each tune. Experiment with different bowings. You will find that in the tunes that follow some bowings work better than others. The more you watch and listen to other fiddlers, the easier it will become to develop a good bowing style of your own. Listen to the recordings listed for the tunes every once in a while, to make sure that you haven't gone too far off the track

Old Molly Hare

Learned from Frank George of Bluefield, West Virginia.

Traditional Music for Banjo, Fiddle and Bagpipes Kanawha 307

To the Beginning

Don Tremaine's Reel

Reels played up-tempo for dances are called *breakdowns* or *hoedowns*.

Tom McCreesh and Jay Ungar team up for a great twin fiddle version of this tune on *The Hammered Dulcimer* (FHR-01).

A Part

B Part

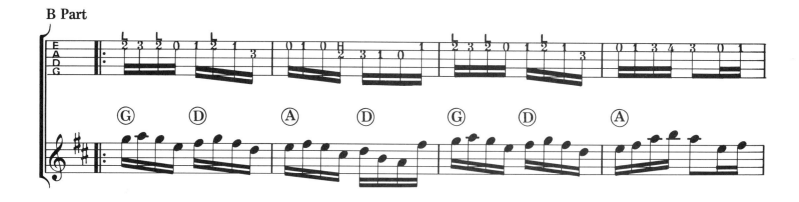

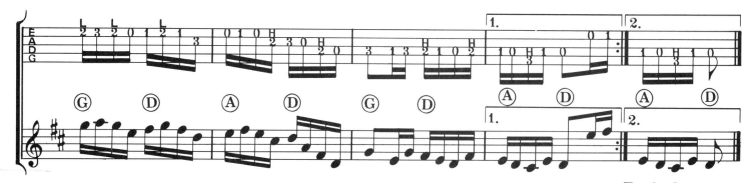

To the Beginning

48

Tunes in the Key of G

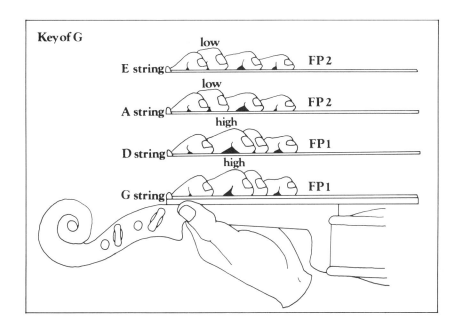

Stoneman's Mountaineers

Cotton Eyed Joe

Here's "Cotton Eyed Joe" as played by Earl Collins:

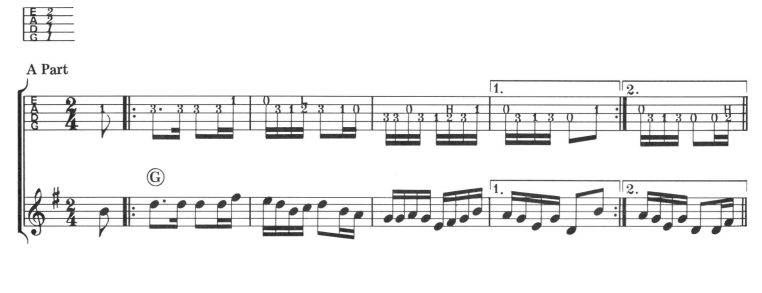

That's Earl Briar 4204

To the Beginning

Magpie

To the Beginning

Fuzzy Mountain String Band Rounder 0010

Sandy River Belle

Sandy River Belle, going to leave you,
Sandy River Belle, going to leave you,

Sandy River Belle, going to leave you,
Going away to leave you now.

Mountain Songs (Dad Blackard's Moonshiners) County 504

Old Mother Flanagan

Kenny Hall and the Sweets Mill String Band Bay727

53

Round Town Gals

This variation of the well-known tune "Buffalo Gals" was recorded in the twenties by a super old-time band known as The Hill Billies.

To the Beginning

Roundtown girls, won't you come out tonight,

Won't you come out tonight,

Won't you come out tonight?

Roundtown girls, won't you come out tonight,

And dance by the light of the moon?

The Hill Billies County 405

Quadrille

An **X** in tab indicates a pause (called a *rest*) during which no music is played. The duration of this pause is indicated in the tab in the same way used for regular notes (𝄽, 𝄾, 𝄿, etc.). Corresponding symbols in standard notation are: 𝄽 𝄾 𝄿

A Part

American Fiddle Tunes Library of Congress AFS L62

To the Beginning

Notice that in the next arrangement the third finger on the D string is often played along with the first finger on the A string. This effect—playing on two strings simultaneously—is known as a *double stop*.

Most double stops found in fiddle tunes consist of harmony notes added to the basic melody, thus giving the tunes a greater sense of fullness.

Other types of double stops are the octave and unison notes which we discussed earlier (see pp. 39 and 41).

Nancy Rowland

This tune, like the others, is in AABB form. The third line here, the "B-Part Variation," can be substituted for the other B Part at any point in your playing of the tune.

Echoes Of The Ozarks, Vol. 3 (The Carter Brothers and Son) County 520

Had a little dog and his name was Rover,
When he died, he died all over.

Had me a wife and she was a Quaker,
She wouldn't work and I wouldn't make her.

In the next tune, "Ebenezer," the slanted line preceding the first note in the fourth measure of the A Part is known as a *slide.*

This is a fairly common fiddling technique in which you slide one of your fingers on the string up the fingerboard (toward the bridge) and then come to rest on the designated note.

You should slide up from the finger position just below the note you are sliding to. To play the slide in this tune, put your third finger down on the space normally used for a high second-finger note and then slide it into its proper place.

To make sure you've got it down, listen to the tune as it is played on the insert record.

Charlie Poole with the North Carolina Rumblers

Ebenezer

Learned from the Fuzzy Mountain String Band (Rounder 0010). Kahle Brewer plays a beautiful, lilting version of this tune called "West Virginia Highway" on *Ernest V. Stoneman and the Blue Ridge Corn Shuckers* (Rounder 02144).

A Part

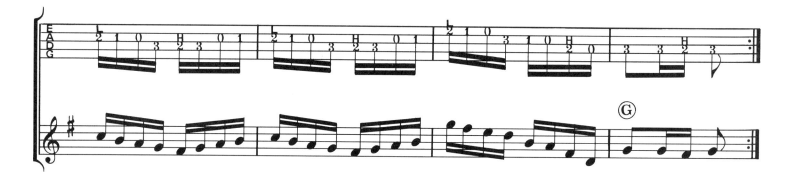

B Part

To the Beginning

Tunes in the Key of A

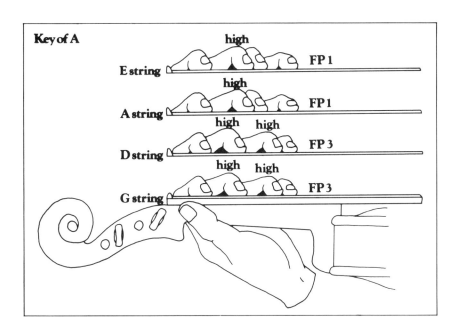

Tony Alderman, John Hopkins, Charlie Bowman, Al Hopkins

Sally Goodin (Fancier Version)

Here's a fancier version of a tune which you should already know well:

A Part

B Part

To the Beginning

A-Part Variation *(may be substituted for A Part)*

Bill Cheatem

This version is based on the fiddling of A.L. Steeley on an old 78 by The Red-Headed Fiddlers.

To the Beginning

Little Rabbit

Learned from a recording of Crockett's Kentucky Mountaineers.

To the Beginning

The Wonderful World of Old Time Fiddlers, vol. 1. Vetco LP104

Steamboat Quickstep

Here's another fine tune in 6/8 time.

Art Rosenbaum and Al Murphy Meadowlands MS-2

My Own House

This is a waltz tune in 3/4 time. The symbol 3/4 means that there are three quarter-note beats (or the equivalent in other notes) to each measure.

The tempo at which fiddlers play waltzes varies across the country. For example, Western fiddlers prefer to play their waltzes slow, while Southeastern fiddlers fancy them at brisker speeds.

A Part

B Part

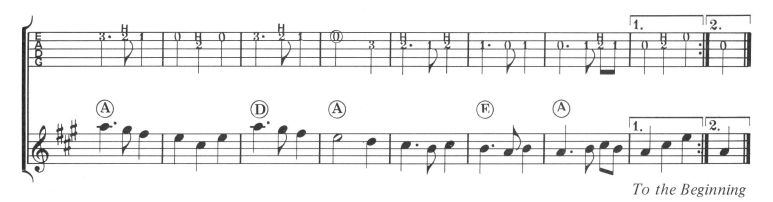

Fire on the Mountain (The Highwoods String Band) Rounder 0028

Mike Seeger

Tunes in the Key of C

Before you try to play tunes in the key of C, you should become familiar with the *fourth finger pattern* (FP4).

The only difference between the second and fourth finger patterns is in the placement of the first finger.

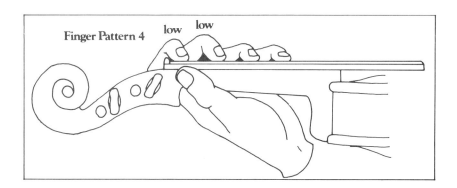

Here your index finger is in low position—next to the nut. Play this pattern through a few times until you get the hang of it.

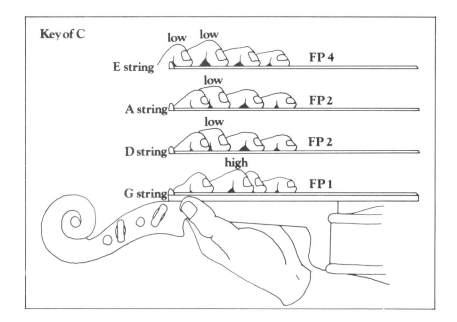

Tunes in the key of C aren't nearly as numerous as those in D, G, and A. But any fiddler worthy of the title usually has a couple of them in his repertoire.

Four Cent Cotton

From a recording of the Skillet Lickers, a wild and zany North Georgia band led by fiddlers Gid Tanner and Clayton McMichen.

A Part

B Part

To the Beginning

The Skillet Lickers County 506

Goin' up the road, whoopin and a holl'rin,
I got drunk on four cent cotton.

Woke up this morning feeling kind of rotten,
I'd been drunk on four cent cotton.

Times is hard, they're getting kind of rotten,
Everybody's selling four cent cotton.

"Who's your favorite fiddler?" I must have been asked that question thousands of times. The strange thing is that I never seem to give the same answer twice. Just when I've found a recording of a fiddler who's won me over, I'm sure to shortly thereafter find another who's equally fascinating. If I were asked that question right now, I guess the answer would be Lowe Stokes. Here's his version of "Billy in the Lowground":

Billy In The Low Ground

This transcription is a bit unusual in that the A and B parts each have an extra measure. Remember that in the key of C, the first finger on the E string is played in low position.

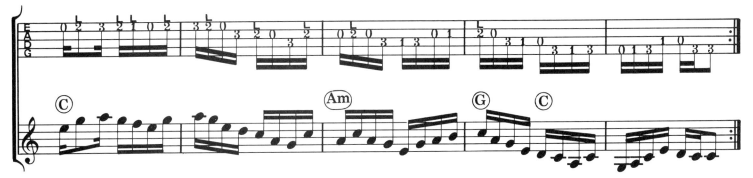

To the Beginning

A Day in the Mountains—1928 The Fiddlin' Bootleggers County 512

Lowe Stokes and his North Georgians

Rocky Pallet

"Rocky Pallet" is sometimes played with an added C Part. But the fiddler who taught it to me only knew two parts to the tune—so that's the way I play it.

A Part

B Part

The Skillet Lickers, vol. 2 County 526

To the Beginning

70

Tunes in More Than One Key

All the tunes that you've learned this far stay in the same key from beginning to end. But there's a whole bunch of fine tunes in which the key changes. Usually this occurs midway through the tune, with the A part in one key and the B part in another.

Franklin George of Union County, West Va. and Alan Jabbour of Washington, DC

Muddy Roads

The late Gaither Carlton of Deep Gap, North Carolina is responsible for the current popularity of this hypnotic melody.

The A part here is in the key of G, while the B part's in D.

A Part

B Part

The Watson Family Folkways FA2356

To the Beginning

Richmond

This version of "Richmond" comes from Henry Reed of Glen Lyn, Va. via Alan Jabbour.

A part—Key of D
B part—Key of A

A Part

B Part

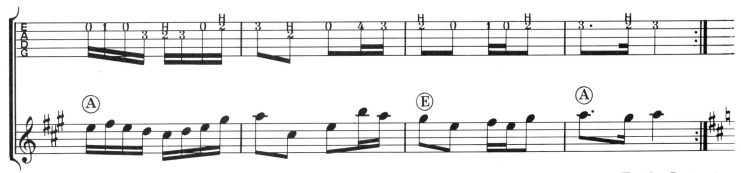

The Hollow Rock String Band Kanawha 311

To the Beginning

Old French

Here's a version of "Old French" derived from the mandolin playing of Kenny Hall. The B part of this tune is actually in the A Mixolydian mode* (A major with a lowered G ($g\natural$) instead of $g\sharp$).

A part—Key of D
B part—Key of A

*See "Modal Tunes," p. 92.

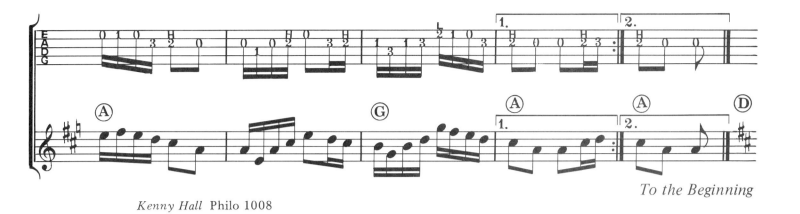

Kenny Hall Philo 1008

Don't limit yourself to learning tunes from fiddlers alone. You can gain some powerful insight into some fiddle tunes from listening to the way mandolinists, banjo players and guitarists play them.

Kyle Creed of North Carolina with friends 1975

Fire On The Mountain

This is one of my all-time favorite tunes.

Notice that the B part consists of ten measures. The last two measures serve to bring the tune around—back to the A part. The B part variation is from a 1928 recording of fiddler Clayton McMichen and Riley Puckett (guitar), *The Wonderful World of Old-Time Fiddlers* (Vetco LP104).

A part—Key of A
B part—Key of D

A Part

B Part

To the Beginning

B-Part Variation

The Wonderful World of Old-Time Fiddlers Vetco LP104

Chorus Jig

"Chorus Jig" isn't really a jig at all, for, as you can see, it's in 2/4 time. The basic structure is AABCCB. This tune is very popular among fiddlers throughout New England.

A part—Key of D
B part—Key of G
C part—Key of D

A Part

B Part

2nd time back to the beginning
Final time end here.

C Part

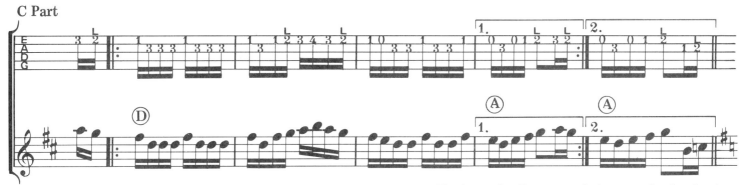

Back to the B part and then to the beginning

Allan Block and Ralph Lee Smith   Meadowlands MS-01

Clayton McMichen 1964

Coin Du Ciel

"Coin du ciel" is French for "a corner of heaven." This version is based on the fiddling of Louis Riendeau of Berlin, New Hampshire. Note that the tab symbol ① indicates a half-note (two beats), and ①• a dotted half-note (three beats).

A part—Key of D
B part—Key of A

A Part

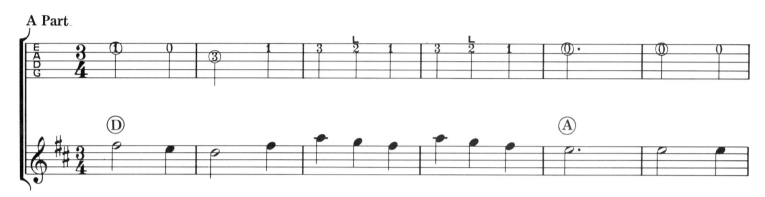

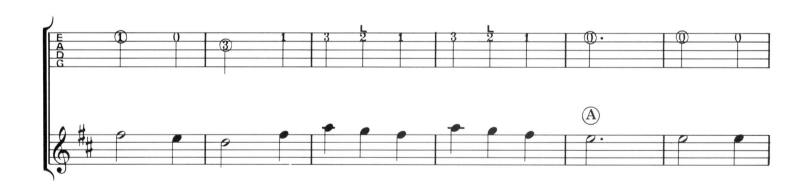

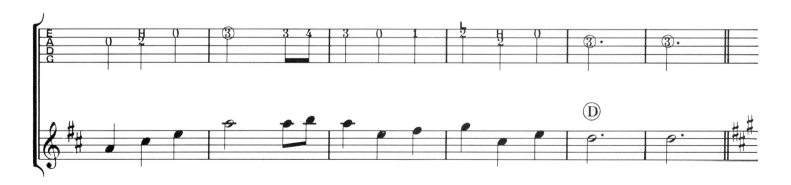

B Part

The Riendeau Family County 725

To the Beginning

Cross Keys

In order to achieve certain effects in his tunes, the old-time fiddler often employs tunings other than the standard violin tuning which we've been using. Most fiddlers refer to these other tunings as *cross key* or *discord* tunings.

For the next tune, "Shootin' Creek," raise your G string one whole step to an A (an octave lower than the A string). Your fiddle should now be tuned:

Some Appalachian fiddlers refer to this tuning as *high bass/low counter,* with "bass" and "counter" referring to the G and D strings respectively.

"Shootin' Creek" is in the key of D. However, since your G string has been re-tuned, you should use the following fiddle-tab key signature in place of the one normally used for this key:

Remember that while the standard notation always shows how the music *sounds*, the tab shows how it's *played.* So a new tuning changes the relationship of tab to standard, for example, with the G string tuned up to an A, a 1 in the tab now means *b* rather than *a.*

The first setting in the following transcription involves the use of only the E, A, and D strings. The variation that follows is a restatement of the basic melody an octave lower, which gives the re-tuned G string a real workout. (Don't break up the A and B Parts of the variation here.)

Notice that now we're using the FP1 on the G string instead of FP3. This makes the tune much easier to finger.

Shootin' Creek

Tuning:

A Part

B Part

To the Beginning

A-Part Variation

B-Part Variation

Fuzzy Mountain String Band Rounder 0010

To the Beginning

Another basic cross-key tuning in the key of D is:

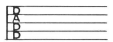

To get into this tuning, lower your G string down to the D an octave below the D string. Then lower your E string to the D an octave above the D string. Both the D and A strings stay the same.

Two tunes commonly associated with this tuning are "Midnight on the Water" (*Benny Thomasson,* County 724), and "Bonaparte's Retreat" (*American Fiddle Tunes,* Library of Congress AFS L62).

The cross-key tuning (in the key of A) for this next tune, "Going Down the River," is as follows:

To put your fiddle into this tuning, tune your G string up as you did for "Shootin' Creek." Then raise your D string one whole step up to the E note an octave lower than your E string. This is known as *high bass/high counter* tuning.

The fiddle-tab key signature for this tuning is:

Notice that FP1 is used here for *all four* strings.

Going Down The River

As played by J.P. Fraley of Rush, Kentucky.

Tuning:

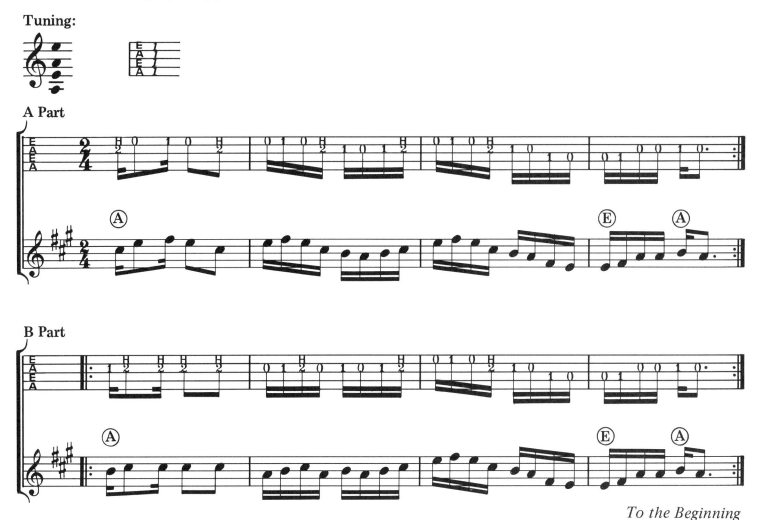

To the Beginning

Oh, my little girl, if you don't do better,
Put you on a boat, gonna send you down the river.
Boat began to sink, my heart began to quiver,
Oh, my little girl, you're goin' down the river.

Here's a variation of "Going Down The River" using *drone strings*. Drones are open strings which are played continuously along with the basic melody, creating a "bagpipe" effect. The use of drones adds further richness and fullness to the sound of the tune.

Playing a tune with drones presents a real challenge to the beginner. On your first attempt with drone tunes you will probably go through the "I sound terrible" stage, but you'll soon get over it—everyone does. The more you work at it, the better you'll sound. But don't try to get over this hurdle by practicing it for hours on end—working on it in small doses is definitely your best bet.

Here are a few things to keep in mind to help you on your way:

1. Arch your fingers so they don't deaden the adjacent drone string.

2. Adjust the angle of your bow so that it rests evenly on both strings. For example, at the very start of the variation, your bow should be resting firmly on both the A and E strings as illustrated below:

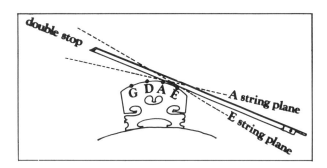

3. As you play, apply even pressure with your bow to each of the two strings.

Play all the 2's in high position here (because of the open drone strings, there is no room for the H's in the tab). The drone part is in italics in the tab and smaller, "cue" notes in standard notation.

Going Down The River (Drone Strings)

Wild Rose Of The Mountain (J.P. Fraley) Rounder 0037

Swing Nine Yards Of Calico

This is another J.P. Fraley tune.

Tuning:

A Part

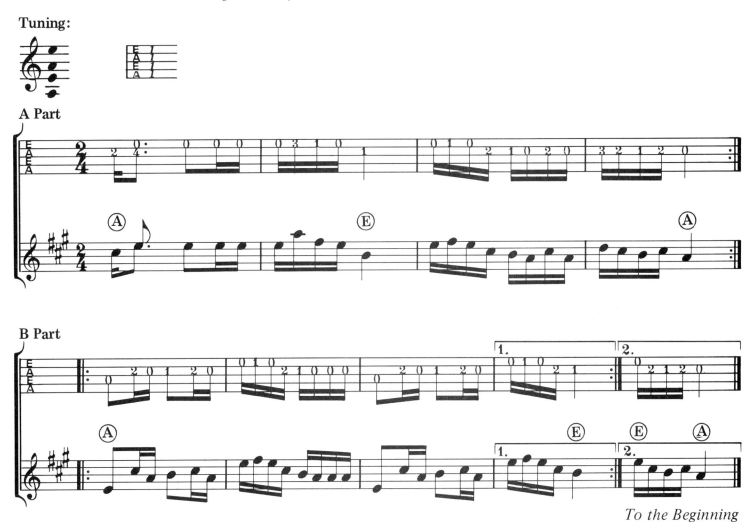

B Part

To the Beginning

Now try to play it with drones. The following chart should provide you with all the information you need for this particular tune:

When melody is on: A string ⟶ Use: E string drone

E string ⟶ A string drone

D (retuned to an E note) ⟶ A string drone

Old Mother Flanagan

Here's a tune we learned way back in the "Key of G" section. The version transcribed here is in an A cross-key tuning. It's amazing how different a tune feels when it is played in a different key. But don't just take my word for it—check it out for yourself.

Tuning:

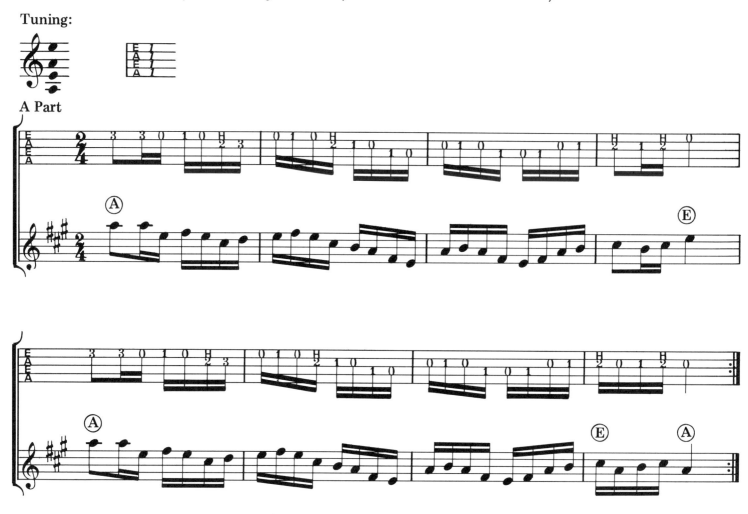

A Part

B Part

The Fuzzy Mountain String Band Rounder 0010

Another tuning used for the key of A is:

This is known as "Black Mountain Blues tuning."

To get this tuning from AEAE, simply lower your E string down to the note (c♯) that matches with the high second finger on your A string.

The Balfa Brothers

Modal Tunes

Modal tunes are a weird bunch; haunting and beautiful all at the same time. They're very lonesome sounding and, in a way, they might be considered the fiddler's equivalent to the blues.

Although the four tunes in this section all use the fingering for the key of G, they are actually closer to being in the key of A minor. The "A minor in the key signature of G," so to speak, is the *A Dorian mode.* The Dorian mode can be played on other notes as well. There are also other commonly used modes, such as the Mixolydian used for "Old French," p. 74 ("A Major in the key signature of D").

Henry Reed

Hog Eye Man

Hollow Rock String Band Kanawha 311

Loch Lavan Castle

To the Beginning

Betty Likens

A Part

B Part

Hollow Rock String Band Kanawha 311

To the Beginning

Bunch Of Keys

A Part

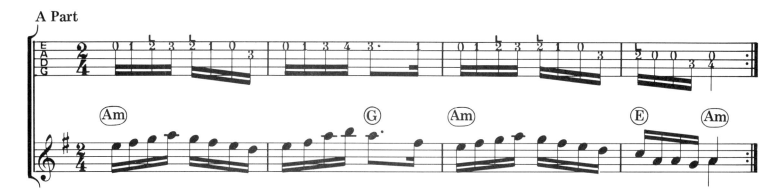

B Part

Pickin' Around the Cookstove Rounder 0040

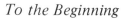
To the Beginning

Melvin Wine of Braxton County, West Va. 1974

96

Boys, My Money's All Gone

Old-Time Fiddle Classics (Charlie Bowman) County 507

The Keys of F and B♭

The Fifth Finger Pattern

The fifth and last finger pattern makes use of a low first finger as well as a low fourth finger, as shown below:

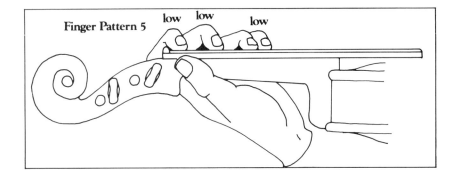

The tab key signature for the key of F is:

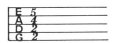

For the key of B♭ it is:

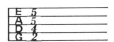

Not too many fiddlers play tunes in F or B♭, for the low first finger in the fourth and fifth finger patterns makes the tunes kind of awkward to play. Some old fiddlers still play "Fisher's Hornpipe" in the key of F. But these days it's most often heard in the key of D. Two great B♭ tunes are "Done Gone" and "The High-Level Hornpipe" (See Christeson's *The Old-Time Fiddlers's Repertory,* Univ. of Missouri Press, p. 32)

Kickoffs and Tags

Kickoffs

A fiddler will often play for a measure or two preceeding the real beginning of the tune. This is known as *kicking off* a tune. A typical old-time kickoff for the key of D is shown below for the tune "Richmond":

This same kickoff can also be done using double stops:

When pickup notes are involved they become absorbed in the kickoff as shown below:

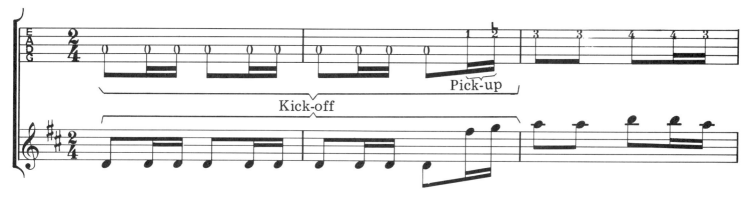

The function of a kickoff is to set the tempo of the tune, as well as to establish the key for the benefit of your accompanists.

Other Kickoffs

For tunes in the key of G:

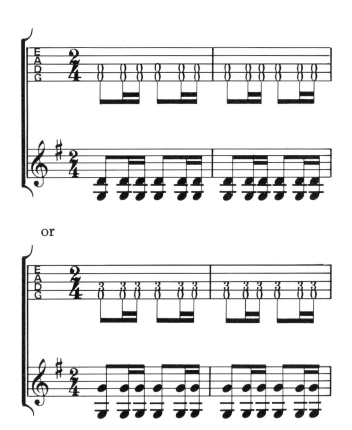

or

For tunes in the key of A:

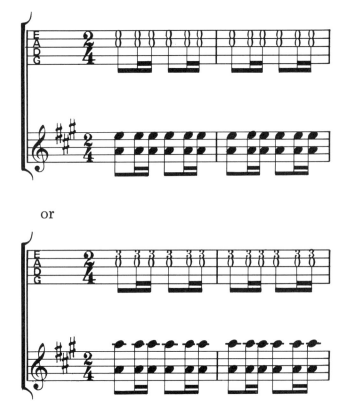

For tunes in the key of C:

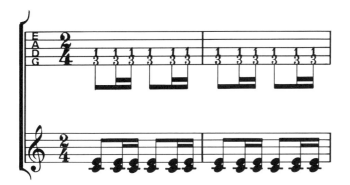

Tags

The notes at the very end of a tune (or part) are known as the *tag*. The most popular of these tags is the "shave and a haircut" shown here for the key of D:

Here are some neat tags for you to fiddle around with:

For the key of D:

For the key of A:

Now try making up some of your own for the tunes you know.

Sherman and Rue Hammons of Marlinton, West Va. 1972

Appendices

APPENDIX I.
CHOOSING A FIDDLE

It's foolish to spend a large sum of money on your first fiddle. But then again you won't want to own a cheap fiddle with a horrible screechy tone that will frustrate you as well as annoy anyone within earshot. Decent fiddles will run you from $50 to about $200. There are no brand names or manufacturers to go by; you just have to keep trying them out until you find one that you really like. I myself prefer copies of German fiddles made from the turn of the century to about the 1940s.

It's a smart idea to take a fiddler along whenever possible to help you try out the instruments.

Where To Look

First look in your attic. You'd be surprised at what some people leave behind or put in storage and then forget about. Ask your family and friends if they know of any violins lying around somewhere not being used.

You might try looking in pawnshops, resell-it shops and in the want ads of your local newspaper. These are but a few of the many places where you are likely to find great bargains.

Ask around. You may find a fiddler with an extra fiddle he is willing to part with for a reasonable price.

Another possibility is renting an instrument. Some music stores will rent you an entire violin outfit (violin, bow, case, and rosin) for a pretty nominal charge. In this way you can start playing right away, and then, when ready to buy an instrument of your own, you will be much more familiar with the instrument, and thus able to make a much more knowledgeable choice.

Bows

A good bow is essential to good fiddling. You can make do with a mediocre fiddle and a good bow, but a combination of a poor fiddle and a poor bow is pretty hopeless. Here again I strongly urge you to get the assistance of a fiddler in picking one out.

APPENDIX II.
CARE AND MAINTENANCE

Here are a few pointers to help you keep your fiddle in good shape:

Strings:

When you're finished playing, it's a good idea to wipe the rosin dust off your strings with a lint-free cloth.

Bow:

Try not to touch the bow-hair with your fingers, as the sweat from your hands will tend to corrode it. Remember to always loosen your bow before putting it away.

Case:

A well-built sturdy case is absolutely essential to maintaining your instrument in good condition. Plywood hardshell cases are your best bet—combining optimum protection with good looks. Your fiddle should fit pretty snugly in its case. If your feel that the case gives your fiddle too much room to move around in, try further padding it with a pillow case or a soft towel. Make sure that the inside of the case has a soft lining with no screws, bolts, or rivets protruding through the lining.

Temperature/Humidity

Keep your fiddle away from any excesses of temperature or humidity. For example, don't store your fiddle near a steampipe or radiator, or in a damp basement.

One further note: keep an eye on your fiddle at all times. Fiddles, being small and easy to walk away with, are prime targets for thieves. If your instrument is of great material value you may want to have it insured.

APPENDIX III.
MORE ON TUNING

One of the most handy portable tools for tuning is the *tuning fork*. The kind that you should use is known as an "A440," so called because it vibrates at 440 cycles per second, thus giving you a standard A note for tuning your fiddle. Tuning forks are inexpensive and can be purchased at most music stores.

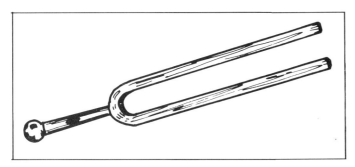

To use one, hold the fork by its long stem and tap one of the U-shaped prongs on a fairly hard surface. Then position the prongs close to your ear and listen. Now, tune your A string to this pitch.

Once you've done this, you can tune up your E string. As an aid to doing this I use the well-known popular melody, "Twinkle, Twinkle, Little Star." Any tune beginning with the same interval (an upwards leap of a fifth—A to E here) will do. I tune by singing the first "twinkle" to the sound of the open A string, then tuning the E string to match the sound of the second "twinkle."

```
  a   a        e   e       f♯  f♯  e
Twinkle,     Twinkle,      Little Star
  ↑            ↑
[A string]   [E string]
```

To tune your D string, you might sing the very first note of the "Star Spangled Banner" to the sound of your A string. Then tune your D string to the sound of the second word (third note) of the anthem.

```
  a    f♯   d   f♯   a    d
O  -  oh   Say  Can  You  See
  ↑         ↑        ↑
[A string] [D string] [A string]
```

Now, to tune the G string follow this same procedure, only this time starting with the D string.

```
  d     b     g    b     d     g
O  -   oh    Say  Can   You   See
  ↑          ↑          ↑
[D string]  [G string]  [D string]
```

Now you should have your fiddle tuned to what is known as standard pitch. Some fiddlers prefer to tune their instruments a little above or below standard pitch. Tuning your fiddle a little lower will make it sound deeper and mellower, while tuning it higher makes the tone sound louder and crisper.

Another device for tuning is the *pitch pipe*, consisting of four reeds, one for each open string. After considerable use, however, the reeds will probably bend out of tune, rendering it quite useless. If you ask me, I'd say to stick with the tuning fork.

You can tune your fiddle to any *other instruments* (provided they are already in tune) once you have determined which of its notes correspond to the open strings of your fiddle.

When tuning to a piano use the chart below:

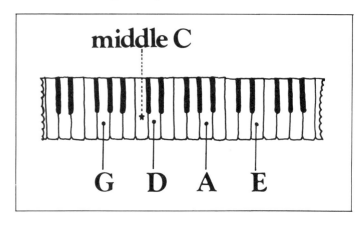

With a guitar:

Fiddle	Guitar
E	E (1st) string at 12th fret
A	B (2nd) string at 10th fret
D	D (4th) string at 12th fret
G	A (5th) string at 10th fret

Some Problems Commonly Encountered With Tuning

Changing tension

Let's say you start out by tuning your G string and then follow with your D, A, and E strings in that order. By the time you have finished tuning your E, you may find that the rest of the strings have gone out of tune. The reason for this is: When you tune up a string you are applying a considerable amount of tension to the belly of the fiddle (via the bridge). As you tune each successive string the tension changes slightly, so that by the time you have tuned all four strings you may then have to go back, repeating the procedure a few times until the tension is equalized.

New strings

When putting on a new set of strings be aware that they will be slipping out of tune for a day or so until they stretch and adjust to the proper tension.

APPENDIX IV.
CHANGING STRINGS

When putting on a new set of strings be sure to replace the old ones one at a time. Always have four strings on the fiddle. In that way you can maintain fairly constant tension on your fiddle, thus making it much easier to tune.

Place the ball end of the string in the hook of the fine tuner. Then align the string in its proper notches on the bridge and the nut. Now pass the threaded end of the string through the hole in the peg. Then turn the peg while keeping the string against the nearest wall of the peg box.

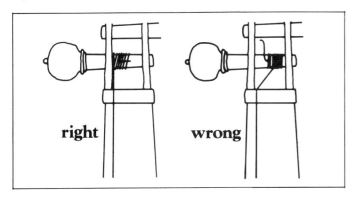

right   **wrong**

If the string has a loop end (which most E strings do) place the loop around the hook (or one of the prongs of the hook) of the fine tuner.

If you haven't had the chance to acquire fine tuners yet, place the ball end of the string through its appropriate hole in the tailpiece. Then, placing your finger over the hole, pull the string, forcing it into the groove adjoining the hole. Follow the same procedure described above for the peg.

If you have loop-ended strings and no fine tuners, thread the string through the loop as illustrated below and then pull the string. Here again, follow the rest of the procedure as discussed above.

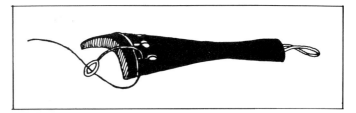

APPENDIX V.
SOME FURTHER TIPS ON FIDDLING TECHNIQUE

Here are some additional notes which will augment our study of technique.

Vibrato

Some fiddlers frown upon the use of vibrato in old-time fiddling, while others go crazy over it, especially with their arrangements of slow, "drippy" waltzes.

The basic concept of vibrato involves rocking the finger back and forth on a note, giving the tone an undulating quality. It's most often used in waltzes where you're likely to have many long sustained notes.

Flattened Bridge Arch

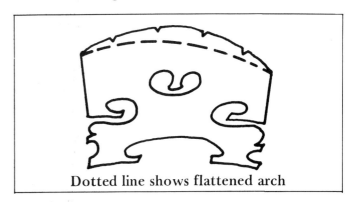

Dotted line shows flattened arch

Many fiddlers prefer to have their bridges less rounded than those used by classical violinists. These flatter bridges make it easier to move your bow from one string to the next, as well as facilitating the playing of drones and double stops.

Play on a few fiddles with flat bridges when you have the chance, and see how you like them. If you would prefer to have the bridge on your fiddle a little flatter, trace the arch of a flat bridge to your liking onto a sheet of paper. Then bring it (along with your fiddle) to a violin-maker or an instrument repairman, who will take it from there and make the adjustment for you.

APPENDIX VI.
FIDDLE TAB AND STANDARD NOTATION
The following chart shows the relationship between fiddle tab and standard notation:

APPENDIX VII.
LOOSENING UP EXERCISES

After a few hours of playing you may feel that some parts of your body have become especially tense. In this situation the best thing to do is stop and relax—and then do a few exercises to help rid you of the tension.

Here are a few exercises which I've found to be especially helpful:

While sitting down on a chair, lower the upper part of your body so that your neck, shoulders, and head are hanging freely, as in the illustration below. Hold on to your ankles with your hands as you do this. Now take a deep breath and exhale; as you do so, imagine that all the tension is draining out of your body. Then slowly raise the upper part of your body to assume your normal sitting posture. Try not to do this exercise for too long at first, as it might make you feel dizzy and nauseous.

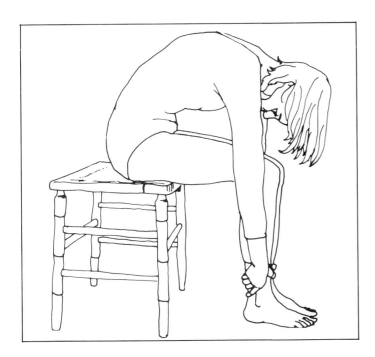

If you feel a great deal of tightness in the muscles surrounding your neck, try the following exercise for some quick relief:

While keeping your back straight, lower your head as far as it will naturally fall. Then slowly begin to move your head in a wide circle, moving in a clockwise direction; to the left, up, to the right and back down again. Continue in this direction a few more times and then try doing it counter-clockwise.

For removing tension from your arms and shoulders try this next exercise:

While extending your arms out at your sides, clench your fists as hard as you can. Hold it for a count of five and then release. Repeat the exercise a few times through.

107

For cramped, tense fingers try the following:

Hold your hands out in front of you with the palms facing you. Make as tight a fist as you possibly can. Hold for a count of five, then slowly open both hands until each digit is fully extended. Repeat through a few times.

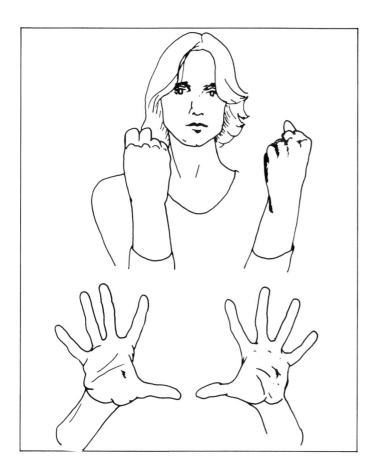

APPENDIX VIII.
GOING FURTHER: BOOK AND RECORD COLLECTION

It always seems that the more you learn, the more you find there is to learn. Boy, is this ever true with old-time fiddling—no matter how many great tunes you've learned, you can rest assured that there are plenty more where they came from.

The following book and record lists are a rich source of old-time fiddle material. As you play new tunes, try to keep a list of them—in that way you'll find them much easier to recall on short notice.

Things To Read

The periodicals listed below feature fine articles on old-time fiddlers and fiddling and are definitely all worth subscribing to.

Devil's Box
Tennesse Valley Old-Time Fiddler's Ass'n.
Route 4, Madison, Alabama 35758

(In each issue of *Devil's Box* you will find a couple of fine tunes transcribed into fiddle tab by Frank Maloy. Don't miss them, they're really excellent!)

JEMF Quarterly
John Edwards Memorial Foundation
Folklore and Mythology Center
University of California
Los Angeles, Cal.

Old Time Music
33 Brunswick Gardens
London W8 4AW, England
(also available from Rounder Records)

Miles Krassen's book *Appalachian Fiddle* (Oak) contains some wonderful Southern tunes along with a very informative section on double stops.

Other tune collections (transcribed in standard notation only!) which you may desire for your own personal library are:

R.P. Christeson's *The Old-Time Fiddler's Repertory*, Univ. of Missouri Press.

O'Neill's Music of Ireland/Revised, Oak Publications.

Basic Record Collection

Peter Feldman has recently completed a series of fiddle instruction records for the Sonyatone label. Each of these fine records is accompanied by a descriptive booklet with fiddle tab. This is highly recommended for those looking for additional instruction on the beginner level.

The following two records are especially recommended for those who wish to further enrich their repertoire with a bunch of fine old-time tunes:

County 756 *Tommy Jarrell—Sail Away Ladies*
Library of Congress AFS L62 *American Fiddle Tunes*

This last record comes with a fifty-odd page booklet providing rich documentation and background information on the tunes.

You can use the following list to help you in making your own basic collection:

Label	Album	Style	Comments
County 756	*Tommy Jarrell—Sail Away Ladies*	Galax	There are very few fiddlers I know of who can move a bow like Tommy can. He's probably one of the most exciting fiddlers around today. This album of unaccompanied fiddle tunes is a treasure.
County 724	*Benny Thomasson*	Texas	One of the most imitated and highly respected of the modern Texas fiddlers.
Swallow 6011	*The Balfa Bros. Play Traditional Cajun Music*	Cajun	Melodies of the bayou country played by a widely acclaimed Louisiana string band.
Kanawha 307	*Frank George—Traditional Music For Banjo, Fiddle And Bagpipes*	W. Va. and Indiana	This album of fine tunes as played by Frank George has become a classic among old-time fiddling enthusiasts. It also features the fiddling of the late John Summers of Marion, Indiana.
Rounder 0037	*J.P. and Annadeene Fraley—Wild Rose of the Mountain*	Kentucky	J.P. Fraley's fiddle style is smooth and soothing, one might even say healing. This particular record always seems to cheer me up when ever I feel down in the dumps.
County 725	*Riendeau Family*	New England	New England tunes with a French Canadian flair. "Louie's First Tune" places pretty high on my list of favorite tunes.
County 526	*The Skillet Lickers, Vol. 2*	North Georgia	Wild, zany, and highly spirited music with beautiful twin fiddle harmonies.
Rounder 0010/ 0035	*Fuzzy Mountain String Band*	Appalachian	A diverse collection of Appalachian tunes as played by a capable young Southern string band. Lots of great modal tunes.
County 517	*Texas Farewell*	Texas	Consists of recordings of Texas fiddlers made between 1922 and 1930 including such groups as The East Texas Serenaders and The Red-Headed Fiddlers.
County 518-520	*Echoes Of The Ozarks*	Ozarks	This three-record set is in my opinion probably the best collection of tunes in the entire County series. Ten points to anyone who can figure out all the words to the Carter Bros. And Son version of "Cotton Eyed Joe."
County 528/529	*Traditional Fiddle Music of Mississippi, vols. 1&2*	Mississippi	This amazing two-record set features the haunting sound of Freeny's Dance Band as well as the bluesy sound of Floyd Ming And His Pep Steppers.
Rounder 0045	*Highwoods String Band—Dance All Night*	North Ga.-Galax	One of the finest city-bred old-time bands at their best.
Vetco 104/106	*The Wonderful World Of Old Time Fiddlers, Vols 1&2*	Anthology	A very listenable and well-put-together anthology which I recommend highly.
Library of Congress AFS L62	*American Fiddle Tunes*	Anthology	Twenty-eight unaccompanied fiddle solos drawn from the Archives Of Folk Song of the Library of Congress

County 507/531	*String Band Classics* (*Old Time Fiddle Classics* and *Old-Time String Band Classics*)	Anthology	As the title implies, classic recordings from the twenties and early thirties by such greats as Eck Robertson, Lowe Stokes and Clayton McMichen.
Folkways 2952	*American Folk Music Anthology, vol. 2*	Anthology	Jilson Setters, Bunt Stephens, G.B. Grayson are but a few of the many great fiddlers represented in this classic reissue.
Historical HLP 8005	*Charlie Poole, 1926-1930*		A fascinating recording of this legendary banjo player highlighting the fiddling of: Posey Rorer, Lonnie Austin, and Odell Smith.
Kanawha 311	*The Hollow Rock String Band*		The fine fiddling of Alan Jabbour, on an album featuring the tunes of the late Henry Reed of Glen Lyn, Va.
Bay 203	*Jody Stetcher— Snake Baked A Hoecake*		One of the most beautiful records of any type that I've ever come across. I totally wore out my copy in no time at all.

ADDITIONAL DISCOGRAPHY *

Some of these records might be hard to find in your local music stores, but they can be ordered from the companies listed. In addition, these companies will be happy to send you their extensive catalogues upon request:

Roundup Records
Box 474
Somerville, Massachusetts 02144
(Enclose 25¢ for postage and handling.)

County Records
P.O. Box 191
Floyd, Va. 24091

BAY RECORDS

203	Jody Stetcher—Snake Baked A Hoecake
727	Kenny Hall—Sweets Mill String Band

COUNTY RECORDS

401	The Stripling Brothers
405	The Hillbillies
505	Charlie Poole
506	Gid Tanner and the Skillet Lickers
507	Old Time Fiddle Classics
509	Charlie Poole, vol. 2
512	A Day In The Mountains 1928
513	Grayson And Whitter
514	Hell Broke Loose In Georgia
516	The Legend of Charlie Poole
517	Texas Farewell
518	Echoes Of The Ozarks, vol. 1
519	Echoes Of The Ozarks, vol. 2
520	Echoes Of The Ozarks, vol. 3
524	DaCosta Woltz Southern Broadcasters
525	Fiddlers Convention in Mountain City, Tenn.
526	Skillet Lickers, vol. 2
528	Traditional Fiddle Music of Mississippi, vol. 1
529	Traditional Fiddle Music of Mississippi, vol. 2
531	Old-Time String Band Classics 1927-1933
536	Kessinger Brothers
540	Charlie Poole, vol. 4
703	Texas Hoedown
705	Virginia Breakdown
707	Texas Fiddle Favorites
724	Benny Thomasson
725	Riendeau Family
756	Tommy Jarrell—Sail Away Ladies

DAVIS UNLIMITED

33015	Fiddlin' Doc Roberts

ELECTRA

7292	String Band Project

FOLK LEGACY

17	Hobart Smith

FOLKWAYS

2325	Mike Seeger—Old Time Country Music
2366	Doc Watson and Family
2395	New Lost City Ramblers, vol. 5
2396	New Lost City Ramblers, vol. 1
2397	New Lost City Ramblers, vol. 2
2398	New Lost City Ramblers, vol. 3
2399	New Lost City Ramblers, vol. 4
2434	37th Old Time Fiddler's Convention

2435	Galax, Virginia Fiddle Contest
2436	Berkeley Farms
2951	American Folk Music Anthology, vol. 1
2952	American Folk Music Anthology, vol. 2
2953	American Folk Music Anthology, vol. 3
3811	Traditional Music of Grayson and Carroll Counties, Va.
3832	Band Music of Grayson and Carroll Counties Va.
31007	McGee Bros. and Fiddlin Arthur Smith—Milk 'Em In The Evening Blues
31039	Red Clay Ramblers with Fiddlin Al McCanless

FRONT HALL

01	Bill Spence—The Hammered Dulcimer
03	Canterbury Orchestra—Swinging on a Gate
05	Fennigs All-Star String Band—Saturday Night In The Provinces

HISTORICAL RECORDS

8005	Charlie Poole 1926-1930

JOHN EDWARDS MEMORIAL FOUNDATION (J.E.M.F.)

103	Paramount Old-Time Tunes

KANAWHA

301	French Carpenter—Elzic's Farewell
307	Frank George—Traditional Music For Banjo, Fiddle & Bagpipes
311	Hollow Rock String Band

LIBRARY OF CONGRESS

L62	American Fiddle Tunes
S-1565	The Hammons Family

MEADOWLANDS

01	Alan Block and Ralph Lee Smith
02	Art Rosenbaum and Al Murphy

OLD TIMEY

100	The String Bands, vol. 1
101	The String Bands, vol. 2

PHILO

1008	Kenny Hall
1023	Jay And Lyn Ungar
2000	Louis Beaudoin

RCA VICTOR

LPV507	Smokey Mountain Ballads
LPV552	Early Rural String Bands

ROUNDER

0010	Fuzzy Mountain String Band
0018	Shaking Down The Acorns
0023	Highwoods String Band
0032	Buddy Thomas
0035	Fuzzy Mountain no. 2
0037	J.P. and Annadeene Fraley
0040	Pickin' Around The Cookstove
0045	Highwoods String Band—Dance All Night
0047	Wilson Douglas
1004	Burnett and Rutherford
1005	Gid Tanner and the Skillet Lickers
1008	Stoneman's Blue Ridge Corn Shuckers
1010	Ed Haley
3003	Putnam County String Band

SWALLOW

6011	The Balfa Bros. Play Traditional Cajun Music

VANGUARD

VRS9147	Old Time Music At Newport (1963)
VRS9183	Traditional Music at Newport, part 2

VETCO

104	The Wonderful World Of Old Time Fiddlers, vol. 1
106	The Wonderful World Of Old Time Fiddlers, vol. 2

VOYAGER

301	Fiddle Jam Sessions
303	Gid Tanner And The Skillet Lickers
304	More Fiddle Jam Sessions

*This list was compiled in 1977.